CHAMPIONING A PUBLIC GOOD

RHETORIC AND DEMOCRATIC DELIBERATION
VOLUME 32

EDITED BY CHERYL GLENN AND STEPHEN BROWNE
THE PENNSYLVANIA STATE UNIVERSITY

Co-founding Editor: J. Michael Hogan

EDITORIAL BOARD:

Robert Asen (University of Wisconsin–Madison)
Debra Hawhee (The Pennsylvania State University)
J. Michael Hogan (The Pennsylvania State University)
Peter Levine (Tufts University)
Steven J. Mailloux (Loyola Marymount University)
Krista Ratcliffe (Marquette University)
Karen Tracy (University of Colorado, Boulder)
Kirt Wilson (The Pennsylvania State University)
David Zarefsky (Northwestern University)

Rhetoric and Democratic Deliberation focuses on the interplay of public discourse, politics, and democratic action. Engaging with diverse theoretical, cultural, and critical perspectives, books published in this series offer fresh perspectives on rhetoric as it relates to education, social movements, and governments throughout the world.

A complete list of books in this series is located at the back of this volume.

CHAMPIONING A PUBLIC GOOD

A CALL TO ADVOCATE FOR HIGHER EDUCATION

CAROLYN D. COMMER

The Pennsylvania State University Press | University Park, Pennsylvania

This volume is published with the generous support of the Center for Democratic Deliberation at the Pennsylvania State University.

Library of Congress Cataloging-in-Publication Data
Names: Commer, Carolyn D., author.
Title: Championing a public good : a call to advocate for higher education / Carolyn D. Commer.
Other titles: Rhetoric and democratic deliberation.
Description: University Park, Pennsylvania : The Pennsylvania State University Press, [2024] | Series: Rhetoric and democratic deliberation | Includes bibliographical references and index.
Summary: "Examines how higher education leaders advanced different public arguments to counter metric- and market-based proposals of the Spellings Commission and makes the case for education as a public good, advocating for college leadership that prioritizes deliberation and offering rhetorical strategies for higher education advocacy"— Provided by publisher.
Identifiers: LCCN 2024000841 |
  ISBN 9780271097336 (hardback) |
  ISBN 9780271097343 (paperback)
Subjects: LCSH: Higher education and state—United States. | Education, Higher—Aims and objectives—United States. | Education, Higher—Social aspects—United States. | Common good. | Rhetoric.
Classification: LCC LC173 .C58 2024 |
  DDC 379.73—dc23/eng/20240125
LC record available at https://lccn.loc.gov/2024000841

Copyright © 2024 Carolyn D. Commer
All rights reserved
Printed in the United States of America
Published by The Pennsylvania State University Press, University Park, PA 16802–1003

The Pennsylvania State University Press is a member of the Association of University Presses.

It is the policy of The Pennsylvania State University Press to use acid-free paper. Publications on uncoated stock satisfy the minimum requirements of American National Standard for Information Sciences—Permanence of Paper for Printed Library Material, ANSI Z39.48–1992.

For my teachers and my students, who have helped me understand why higher education is a public good worth arguing for.

CONTENTS

List of Tables | ix

Preface | xi

Acknowledgments | xiii

Introduction: Higher Education's Public Crisis | 1

1 The Spellings Commission and the Problem of Managerial Style | 15
2 Rivaling Accountability | 39
3 Building a Public Frame | 59
4 Leading for the Public Good | 78
5 A New Rhetoric for Higher Education Advocacy | 102

Epilogue | 121

Appendix | 123

Notes | 125

Bibliography | 141

Index | 151

TABLES

1. Summary of key features of the managerial style | 33
2. Summary of key features of the academic style | 34
3. Comparison of guiding values for the managerial and academic styles | 34
4. Five models of the public sphere commonly invoked in debates about US higher education | 71

PREFACE

In 2013 I led my first delegation of graduate students from Carnegie Mellon University, in Pittsburgh, Pennsylvania, to Washington, DC, for a higher education policy lobbying weekend. We came together from different departments—English, Chemistry, Computer Science, Engineering and Public Policy, and Social and Decision Sciences—to collectively advocate for public funding for graduate education, research support, international student visas, and open-access research. To prepare for our meetings with policymakers, we were prompted to be prepared to answer questions such as, "What makes your research worth funding? How will it serve the public good?" Driving together along the Pennsylvania Turnpike, we discussed our research and practiced giving each other feedback.

Whereas each of us had some practice articulating the value of our research to other faculty and scholars in our fields, none of us had experience making a case for our research's value to a policymaker or public outside of higher education. In the act of explaining how to understand our work as having public value, I discovered that we were not only advocating for the value of graduate education and public research, but that we were, in a way, advocating for the very idea of higher education itself *as a public good.*

Soon after, I served as a legislative director for the National Association of Graduate Students and Professional Students (NAGPS). In assuming my new role, I tried to find books that could help those inside higher education navigate policy scenarios when called on to defend the public value of higher education. But I found few. What I found instead were critiques of the university and manifestos defending the humanities. I also found books that described the public policymaking process in general or that documented the histories of public higher education's decline through increased lack of public funding. Ultimately, what proved most helpful for learning to articulate higher education's public value were the kinds of deliberations we had in the van rides, and with congressional staffers, when we held each other's work accountable to the public knowledge mission of US higher education.

I also found inspiration in studying how past leaders in higher education responded publicly to attacks on higher education, such as during the

Spellings Commission on Higher Education controversy from 2006–7. It was through my study of this pivotal policy case in US education history that I began to understand the situated constraints and challenges of arguing for higher education as a public good in policy contexts when market-based rationales for higher education dominate the agenda. Addressing these situated challenges clarified why we need a new approach to policy deliberation when it comes to higher education policy.

I wrote this book primarily for faculty and graduate students who are, or will someday be, leaders in higher education, and who at some point will be called upon to defend its public significance. My goal is for readers to see how taking up a *rhetorical* approach to higher education advocacy—one that takes seriously the role of language and deliberation in helping to resolve shared problems—can be a meaningful alternative to the many leadership guide books meant for managing higher education today. My hope is that this book serves as inspiration for upholding higher education's public promise.

ACKNOWLEDGMENTS

I have many people and institutions to thank for this book, since it is one outcome of an inquiry that began more than fifteen years ago when I was an undergraduate at the Evergreen State College, where I started my inquiry into the public value of higher education. The majority of the research for this book started when I was a graduate student in Rhetoric at Carnegie Mellon University (CMU) and the writing of this book has continued into my faculty career at Virginia Tech.

First, I am grateful to the faculty in the Department of English at CMU, who helped me to begin formalizing this project when I was a doctoral student. I am indebted to Andreea Ritivoi for enthusiastically supporting this project, even as I struggled to articulate why the Spellings Commission controversy was so important for those interested in the rhetoric of higher education. When others could not see the need for this project in its earliest stages, Andreea could, and her clear vision of it was a great help. I am also indebted to the wisdom and guidance of David Kaufer, who frequently reminded me that good higher education leaders are those who take time to learn from the people in their community and who, as a result of that learning, are able to frame problems and structure the conditions for sound decision-making. For the model of deliberative leadership I begin to outline in this book, I am deeply indebted to Linda Flower, who also taught me how to lead a community think tank and took time to give me detailed feedback about chapter 4. Finally, I want to acknowledge Jeffrey J. Williams for encouraging me to write about higher education policy and leadership, and for offering invaluable professional guidance about publishing long after I graduated CMU.

It was also at CMU that I had the opportunity to work directly on higher education policy and leadership through my role as President of the Graduate Student Assembly (GSA) and as the Vice President for External and Legislative Affairs. I want to thank the GSA Advisory Board, specifically Suzie Laurich-McIntyre, who taught me about the value of working collaboratively and diplomatically across disciplines, hierarchies, and interests in a large research university. I am also grateful to all the graduate students and the National Association for Graduate and Professional Students (NAGPS) for organizing lobbying days and policy training sessions in Washington, DC, where I first began speaking with policymakers about the value of higher education as a public good.

At Virginia Tech (VT) I have had the good fortune of generous colleagues, bright students, and generous institutional support for this book project. I want to thank Kelly Pender and Katrina Powell for their friendship and mentorship. I am especially grateful to Kelly for reading an early version of my book proposal and for giving me the encouragement I needed to send out the proposal for review. I also want to acknowledge VT colleagues and friends who read early drafts of some chapters, specifically Chris Lindgren and Jennifer Sano-Franchini, who helped me reframe its introduction in light of the contemporary moment. A special thanks, too, to the many graduate students who helped shape my ideas for the book in discussions during my Classical and Modern Western Rhetoric seminars held from 2016 to 2021. I want to thank the College of Liberal Arts and Human Sciences at VT for supporting this project through two Niles Research Grants, and the Provost's office, specifically the Office of Faculty Affairs, for sponsoring faculty writing retreats (where I wrote much of this manuscript), and for granting me a teaching release to complete it. I am also grateful for writing support I received from Deanna Stouder—I could not have finished the manuscript without her coaching. As for capable students, I must also thank Molly Ryan, who was a skilled research assistant and helped me to edit and prepare the penultimate version of the manuscript you are reading now.

As a scholar of rhetoric, I am very grateful to the Rhetoric Society of America for being an intellectual home in the development of my scholarship for the last ten years. In particular, I want to thank seminar and workshop leaders at the RSA Institutes, where I received some of the most important and formative feedback on ideas in this book, such as in Going Deep with the New Rhetoric (David Frank, John Gage, James Crosswhite, and Linda Bensel-Myers), Argumentation (David Zarefsky, Jeanne Fahnestock, Jean Goodwin, Robin Rowland, and Frans Hendrik van Eemeren), Rhetoric and Public Policy (Robert Asen), Rhetoric and Economics (Mark Longaker and David Gore), and Rhetorics of Citizenship (Catherine Palczewski and Karma Chávez).

Thanks to Robert Asen for reading and commenting on an early draft of the proposal for this book, and for his encouragement to send it to the Rhetoric and Democratic Deliberation series at Penn State. I also owe much to Scott Wible, an anonymous reviewer, and the faculty advisory board at Penn State University Press, who have all given generous and invaluable feedback on the manuscript. A special thanks to Penn State University Press, series editors

Cheryl Glenn and Stephen Browne, and acquisitions editor Archna Patel, who each provided support for this project and helped it to spring into being.

Finally, I want to thank my family and friends for so patiently supporting me as I researched and wrote this book. In the final stages of drafting the manuscript, I received a great deal of encouragement and feedback from fellow writing collaborators Mary Glavan, Derek Handley, Doug Cloud, and Amanda Tennant. Most of all, I want to acknowledge my partner, Avery Wiscomb, whose steadfast commitment and willingness to read whatever I write has made all the difference. Thank you.

A portion of this book has been published previously elsewhere. Chapter 2, "Rivaling Accountability," is derived in part from my article "Rivaling the Rhetoric of Accountability: Dissociation as an Advocacy Strategy in US Higher Education Policy," *Argumentation and Advocacy* 57, no. 1 (2021): 18–36, copyright © 2021 American Forensic Association, reprinted by permission of Taylor & Francis Ltd on behalf of American Forensic Association.

INTRODUCTION: HIGHER EDUCATION'S PUBLIC CRISIS

Universities need advocates.
—Stefan Collini

In 363 BCE, the ancient Athenian educator Isocrates wrote an imaginary legal defense against the charges of "not paying more of his fair share to the city" and "corrupting the youth." In his treatise *Antidosis*, Isocrates argues that he has done more than his fair share of public service through the civic education he provided the city's youth.[1] Although some of his students have unfortunately gone on to be the politicians who led Athens into disastrous imperial military campaigns, or to use their rhetorical training for personal financial gain in the law courts, he should not be held responsible for the actions of every one of his students. If viewed over the span of his whole life, Isocrates argues, his efforts to provide a civic education and to imbue his students with democratic values and skills in deliberation and oratory have brought more public good to Athens than bad.

Many US college presidents, administrators, and faculty members can probably relate to Isocrates's defense of his civic efforts. Ask anyone in higher education today and they will tell you: higher education is under attack. If you skim the headlines of the *Chronicle of Higher Education* or *Inside Higher Ed* any day of the week, it seems there is now a constant need to defend higher education's value to the public. Popular media and politicians increasingly position colleges as elite sites of "cancel culture" and leftist indoctrination. TV news pundits and Silicon Valley moguls argue that colleges leave students more economically disadvantaged than when they arrive. And outrage peddlers surveil the social media of faculty searching for "gotcha" posts in an attempt to undermine their credibility and, by extension, that of the university. These headlines and mistruths are part of a decades-long attack on the very promise of higher education as a public good and have fueled the public crisis surrounding higher education.[2]

In calling higher education a public good, I mean that it is a type of *social good* "whose benefit continues to increase as it approaches universal access."[3] While definitions of "the public" have been debated since antiquity, in calling something a "public good" we typically intend to ascribe it a positive value that is valuable to the whole of society. But this term is used in more technical ways, too. For example, in economics a "public good" is a good that must be both "nonexcludable" and "nonrivalrous."[4] While in current practice higher education may not operate purely as a public good in the economic sense (it is sometimes excludable and sometimes rivalrous), it has the *potential* to be. If higher education is fundamentally about providing public knowledge, and if that knowledge is nonexcludable and nonrivalrous, then we could argue that higher education is indeed a type of public good.[5] While there has been some debate about whether and how to classify higher education as a public good, these debates are not merely theoretical or philosophical. Our sense of whether higher education is a public good, a private good, or some type of "dual good" matters because that definition has rhetorical and material consequences. To say that higher education is a public good is to lay the groundwork for arguing that higher education should be *valued* like a public good and thus *funded* like one.

For the purposes of this book, I argue that we should think of higher education as a public good insofar as it relies, in principle, on public funding, and that funding necessarily comes with a promise that it will offer benefits (social, political, educational, and economic) to all its members, regardless of whether they actually attend or participate directly in its activities.[6] *This* is higher education's public promise.

But as higher education's public promise and its value as a public good have increasingly been called into question, there has been weakening trust between the public and higher education. This weakening trust has resulted in policy decisions that cut state funding, usually in the name of "accountability." As public higher education institutions receive less and less financial support from state taxpayers, colleges and universities have been criticized more and more for their failure to educate enough students cheaply or quickly or to prepare them with the skills necessary for the United States to compete in a global marketplace, thus intensifying the perceived decline in the value of a higher education degree. As US student loan debt now tops

$1.7 trillion, the issue of holding colleges and universities accountable for justifying their value to the public has become particularly urgent as a policy issue.[7] For many in higher education, the effect of public attacks and calls for more accountability and new metrics with which to hold higher education accountable have had a significant effect on its leadership, ranging from apathy or annoyance to intense anxiety or early retirement.

Similar to Isocrates, leaders in US higher education today find themselves put on the defensive, yet most lack his preparation.[8] It is especially difficult to defend institutions of higher education coherently because our system of higher education includes a broad array of constituencies and a diversity of institution types. As education historian David Labaree argues: "Many of the system's central operating principles—such as extreme organizational complexity, operational opacity, and a strange mix of highbrow knowledge and lowbrow athletics—simply lack face validity."[9] Institutions of US higher education have traditionally maintained a great degree of institutional autonomy; however, increasingly they must be sensitive to "consumers" and other stakeholders who drive current policy initiatives that focus on accountability.

In short, the belief that higher education is and should be funded as a public good is no longer a shared value or assumption, but a controversial position that must be defended and vociferously advocated for in public policy settings.[10] But as any higher education leader can attest, arguing that higher education is an inherent public good—and not just a personal financial investment for individuals—is harder than it seems. There are three primary constraints for that argument.

The first constraint is that our public policy lexicon for higher education is dominated by market terms and vocabulary for defining "value." Consider, for example, the Bill and Melinda Gates Foundation's Postsecondary Value Commission, launched in 2019, which was charged with investigating "what a college degree is worth."[11] The Gates Commission focuses primarily on defining value by quantifying economic impact and job attainment. Though the Commission states equity as a primary goal, it defines equity solely in *economic return on investment*, implicitly removing other aims of education from the question of value. This change in policy discourse matters because it indicates how the language of the marketplace has so thoroughly permeated our approach to policymaking that we seem to have no common language for noneconomic values. The specific terms that the Gates Commission uses also matter because how we define the value of a college degree affects who will have access to it, and what access can do not only in the lives of students but also for the society in which we live.

The second related constraint is that as higher education's value has been defined in market terms, it has been increasingly perceived, funded, and experienced as a *personal* financial investment for students. For example, a recent bulletin from the American Association of Colleges and Universities (AAC&U) reported that while employers largely agree that college degrees are worthwhile, public perceptions of whether the "investment of time and money" in earning a college degree "vary dramatically by income level, educational attainment, and political affiliation." The AAC&U survey found that 73 percent of respondents with a bachelor's degree and 74 percent with an annual income greater than $100K believe the investment in college education to be worthwhile, compared with just 51 percent of respondents who do not hold a college degree and 52 percent with an annual income below $50K.[12] Even studies such as this one from the AAC&U—a major proponent of the liberal arts and humanities in higher education—frame "value" in terms of the personal time and financial investment that students and parents make in relation to potential student earnings. Perhaps more concerningly, such studies also link this to political affiliation, suggesting that public perceptions of higher education's value may be politically polarizing.[13]

The third constraint is that it is difficult to convene and create situations to deliberate about, and to advocate for, higher education's public promise to policymakers with other stakeholders. Unlike K–12 US education policy, which is governed primarily by local school boards,[14] higher education policymaking happens at state and federal levels and is only subsequently implemented top-down at individual institutions. One result of college and university autonomy, akin to departmental autonomy within them, is that it can seem as though there are few, if any, places where deliberation about policymaking issues that will affect all of them can take place. At the same time, the problem of how to advocate for changes to higher education policy is exacerbated by two other distinctive features of colleges and universities in the United States already mentioned: the vast diversity of mission types that comprise "the system" of higher education and a multiplicity of stakeholders and audiences with competing interests and values.[15]

This book begins with the assumption that most higher education policy problems are fundamentally *rhetorical* problems, by which I mean that public policy is always "a mediation of rhetorical and material forces."[16] Policy problems are rhetorical problems because they are marked by uncertainty and require people to use language to appeal to particular audiences, to discover shared values, and to invite others to take particular actions that have material consequences. For decades now, faculty and administrators in higher education have attempted to defend the public value of higher education, especially as policies have been passed that cut public funding and support. But when they have been able to advocate in numbers, there has been a tendency to respond to policy decisions within the discourse of the market ("higher education can make students more competitive in the marketplace"), which narrows the scope and significance of higher education's public promise and mission.

As some policy analysts have begun to note, higher education, and especially its administrators, are often criticized by faculty and others for acting and making decisions like for-profit corporations. And yet, institutions of higher education do *not* act like for-profit corporations when it comes to lobbying for better public funding. To put it in sports terms: higher education advocacy today is all defense, no offense.[17] In this book, I propose that if we wish to ensure higher education's infrastructure for a thriving democracy, then we need to transform our current approach to higher education policy today. We need to change both our advocacy practices and our policy vocabulary so that higher education can be valued and funded as a place for meaningful reflection and growth, a place where people cultivate public capacities for inquiry, a place where people forge commitments to others, and a place where people develop an understanding of democratic responsibilities.

Drawing from my work as a rhetorical scholar, my background as a former legislative policy coordinator, and my experience as an English professor at a public state college where I spend a lot of time talking with students about what makes their education meaningful and valuable to them, this book offers a guide to public policy advocacy for higher education. To do so, it offers examples of the rhetorical strategies and tactics used by advocates who have historically made the case for higher education as a public good to policymakers and wider publics when higher education has been attacked or criticized. This book contributes to recent work in rhetorical studies that focuses on the rhetorical dimensions of education policy, such as Robert Asen's *Democracy, Deliberation, and Education* and Mark Hlavacik's *Assigning Blame: The Rhetoric of Education Reform*. Both of these works have defined the rhetorical history of US higher education policy at the K–12 level, documenting how market-based education reforms have shaped deliberative conditions at the local and federal level.[18] In this book I extend that work specifically to higher education policy contexts. To do so, I analyze advocates' efforts to defend the value of higher education when criticized or questioned in policymaking forums. In particular, I focus on four public arenas where education leaders from across a diversity of institution types (community colleges, Ivies, private liberal arts, HBCUs, public state and land grant colleges, private research universities, etc.) may be expected to provide public responses to policy issues: academic media outlets, institutional and professional organization forums, policy think-tank forums, and government-sponsored policy forums and hearings.[19]

This book argues that to get better at doing public advocacy work, we need to examine pivotal moments when the rhetoric of higher education policy shifted significantly from public to private aims. In particular, we need to examine recent cases when higher education's value has been redefined by market-based metrics of accountability. No greater example of this can be found than the Commission on the Future of Higher Education, also known as the Spellings Commission, which was announced by the U.S. Department of Education on September 19, 2005. Led by U.S. Secretary of Education Margaret Spellings, the Commission was charged by President George W. Bush with recommending a national strategy for reforming postsecondary education, with a particular focus on how well colleges and universities are preparing students for the twenty-first-century workforce. It was composed of nineteen members, including university presidents and faculty, leaders in higher education professional organizations, and top-level executives from the business world such as IBM, Microsoft, Boeing, and Kaplan, Inc. (see appendix). Over a two-year period from 2005 to 2007, the Commission hosted numerous meetings, hearings, and public roundtables for its work, which were reported on the U.S. Department of Education website and culminated with their widely publicized report entitled *A Test of Leadership: Charting the Future of U.S. Higher Education* (known popularly as the Spellings Report).

Released on September 26, 2006, the Spellings Report focused on four key areas for higher education reform, which have largely set the national policy agenda since: access, affordability (particularly for nontraditional students), quality, and the accountability of institutions of higher learning to their constituencies (students, families, taxpayers, and other investors in higher education). The Spellings Report took an unprecedented no-nonsense tone and sharply criticized higher education, sparking one of the greatest public-policy controversies in US higher education history. The controversy surrounding the Spellings Commission forced many higher education leaders and professional associations to assume a more prominent public role in defending higher education's public value. Of all the higher education commission reports in US history, the Spellings Commission report garnered the most public responses and inspired studies of its controversial reception.[20]

For leaders who want to enter into higher education advocacy efforts, I argue that the Spellings case is significant to study because it created a new era of accountability reforms that requires higher education leaders to be responsive to policymakers through market metrics.[21] Throughout the book, I draw from examples of how many in higher education publicly represented higher education's value in response to the Spellings Report's recommendations (either directly or indirectly).[22] I show how higher education advocates have argued for higher education as a public good to make vivid to future advocates not only the wide range of audiences and argument types they will need to engage, but also some of the possible consequences of doing so.

The model of higher education advocacy I derive from these examples and present in the book functions as a guide for approaching three of the most difficult questions facing higher education leaders today:

1. How can we make a strong case to policymakers to uphold higher education's public promise?
2. What is the best way to measure and represent higher education's value as a public good, not just an economic good?
3. How can institutions of higher education help better prepare its leadership with the rhetorical capabilities needed for effective public advocacy in higher education contexts?

Why We Need New Advocacy Models

Of course, public higher education has not been without its advocates or models of advocacy at both the faculty and administrative levels—it is just that they have been ineffective in significantly changing public attitudes and perceptions. The ineffectiveness of advocates, I claim, is largely due to the models they have to draw from, and their adherence to the underlying belief that higher education *is* by that very fact already a public good. For most faculty, the belief that our teaching and research work contributes to the public good is so commonplace, so taken for granted as a basic assumption, that we can hardly imagine the need to defend it as such.

For example, at a roundtable on the public humanities, philosopher Judith Butler described the feeling of many faculty when they explained, "Sometimes I find myself quite incredulous because I mistakenly thought the public value of these activities [of reading, writing, and critical thinking] is so obvious that they hardly needed to be defended."[23] Butler is not alone in feeling incredulous about the current situation of playing defense in higher education. But what should faculty do with this incredulous feeling?

When we in higher education advocate for its public promise, we tend to address those already in it through genres and moralizing arguments they are already familiar with reading and writing, including scholarly monographs, academic research papers, or thought pieces in print and online publications intended largely for us, such as the *Chronicle of Higher Education* or *Inside Higher Ed*.[24] Faculty models for higher education advocacy tend to be addressed to audiences internal to it, or to those inside their fields, and in the genres and modes we are familiar with, rather than outwardly to those who are responsible for making the decisions that shape public funding for higher education or reelecting them: policymakers and the public.

In addition, one recent trend in advocates' responses to higher education's public crises has been to create new fields examining the role of higher education in society, or to write manifestos and critiques of the university that call attention to the waning influence of the liberal arts and humanities in US higher education.[25] Books such as Martha Nussbaum's *Not for Profit: Why Democracy Needs the Humanities* and Michael Roth's *Beyond the University: Why Liberal Education Matters* serve to strengthen adherence to values like critical thinking, open questioning, ethical reasoning, and the importance of the use of narrative in understanding and championing human political and social problems. These books are important for how they articulate a lexicon of values its readers mostly share, and they bring clarity to the humanistic purposes of higher education. But they also tend to be read by and directed primarily at those who are already familiar with such crises and who already adhere to the values promoted by the liberal arts and humanities traditions they teach and defend. Manifestos or defenses are thus not the most effective platforms for engaging external stakeholders or policymakers.[26]

In addition, faculty have also attempted to address the decline in public funding for higher education by carefully chronicling its history and demonstrating its consequences. Typically, they have done so through painstaking historical research and by critiquing policy decisions that have cut public funding for higher education.[27] Ultimately, they offer alternative policy solutions to fix public-funding cuts and the inequities they have either created or made worse. For example, Christopher Newfield's *The Great Mistake: How We Wrecked Public Universities and How We Can Fix Them* and Sara Goldrick-Rab's *Paying the Price: College Costs, Financial Aid, and the Betrayal of the American Dream* call for a recommitment to public funding for higher education and outline specific financial-aid policy and other changes that would widen access to US higher education, especially for first-generation and low-income students. Such books are invaluable for offering historical insight into the practical, technical aspects of policymaking needed to make college more accessible.

But what makes these studies ultimately ineffective as models of advocacy for higher education is their lack of explicitness concerning what those in higher education can effectively *do* when called upon to be public advocates. So, while it is valuable to document the causes of inequity and to critique the consequences of higher education's failure to effectively make the public case for higher education in policy settings, such books seldom address the prior problem that I do here: *How can those in higher education become prepared to make better cases to policymakers when it counts?*

Why Higher Education Leaders Need Better Rhetorical Capabilities

Just as faculty have mostly ineffective models for higher education advocacy, so do most administrators in leadership roles. Their need to lead in difficult times is evident in the "guidebook trend" in book publishing for university leadership, who perhaps more than faculty understand their lack of effectiveness in producing the outcomes they desire for their institutions. For example, recent books published in the Johns Hopkins University Press series Higher Ed Leadership Essentials, such as *How to Run a College, An Insider's Guide to University Administration*, and *How to Be a Dean*, are emblematic of this emerging genre. Both the popularity and the growing number of how-to books point to the felt need for training administrative leadership for more complex roles in managing higher education.[28] However, these guidebooks tend to focus on the increasingly complex technical aspects of successfully running a college in an age of accountability—how to collect assessment data, work with governing boards, and institute performance-based budgeting models—as a matter of course, not necessarily how to engage the public and policymakers *about* these issues.

Some how-to guidebooks also offer explicit models of leadership that could translate well to public work. However, their leadership models for higher education tend to be campus-focused. For example, books such as Brent Ruben et al.'s *A Guide for Leaders in Higher Education: Core Concepts, Competencies and Tools* argue that today's leaders in higher education need to consider the complexity of their jobs according to two metaphorical models for leadership: (1) the higher education leader as organizational ethnographer and (2) the higher education leader as cross-cultural communicator. As organizational ethnographers, university leaders are encouraged to "become students of the various cultures they encounter within the institution—focusing thoughtful attention on observation, listening, and analysis of the behavior and actions of the groups and organizations with whom leaders must work."[29] As cross-cultural communicators, university leaders are encouraged to "value outcomes and process equally" and seek to "emphasize shared goals."[30] While Ruben et al. give tips on how to manage and work with a diverse range of stakeholders within the university, what both metaphors of leadership have in common as models for change is their inward focus on the internal workings of the institution, not necessarily to a wider public beyond the campus.

The Higher Ed Leader as Public Advocate

Making the case for higher education as a public good both inside and outside the university requires a different response than is presently popular, one that goes beyond a messaging campaign run by a university's marketing or PR department—it requires reorientation and responsiveness from faculty, leadership, and administrators to the public work of being educators.[31] It also requires advocates working in the university with rhetorical capabilities, including an understanding of audience, timing, the ability to tell compelling narratives, and the ability to draw on arguments shared across stakeholders that frame the public value of higher education in a way that facilitates changes in public perception and policymaking.

To become more effective advocates of public higher education, we need a different kind of guidance than the organizational charts of stakeholders, budget primers, and tips for structuring meeting agendas. We will also need something different than critiques of the university and histories of higher education and its public gutting, and something more than manifestos defending the liberal arts and humanities. While these types of books are necessary, they do not help faculty and university leaders understand what effective public advocacy work *outside* the university with policymakers and other stakeholders should look like. To truly address higher education's public crisis, we need a third model for how to prepare leaders in higher education today: the higher education leader as *public advocate*.

The higher education leader this book seeks to cultivate is a public advocate who approaches their work not merely in response to public concerns but as an *active co-creator of our shared public life*. In this way, it seeks to help leaders recognize the constitutive role that universities already play in creating our sense of the public good and offers a rhetorical approach for understanding current policy related to accountability efforts and remaking it.

While this type of public advocate should more directly influence education policy than current models and deliberative infrastructure permit, they do not necessarily need to become rhetoricians, policy experts, or cultural historians of higher education or run for public office. This distinction is important since policy experts tend to be professionals "whose authority is built on a claim to mediate an encounter among various forms of power."[32] Instead, the higher education leader as public advocate should be an expert in how to convene, advocate, and deliberate public affairs. Like the story I describe in the preface about taking a group of graduate student researchers to Washington, DC, this type of leadership work is *communal*.

What Is a Rhetorical Approach to Higher Education Advocacy?

Since we have vast and competing, and often even contradictory, desires and hopes for higher education, it should be expected that people will come into conflict in instances of policymaking or deliberating about responses to it. To be an effective advocate for education, higher education leaders need to be able to tell the story of higher education as a public good in many situations and to many different kinds of public stakeholders (faculty, students, trustees, alumni, local government officials, state policymakers, federal policymakers, and more).[33] But rather than a single advocacy narrative that works for "the public," the rhetorical approach to higher education advocacy I advocate for here means developing the rhetorical capabilities we need to understand and adapt to different situations.

To help leaders cultivate these rhetorical capabilities, this book draws inspiration from what are known in the ancient Greek rhetorical tradition as "commonplace arguments" (*topoi*), which form the starting places of public argument because they offer a simple, yet insightful way to teach people how to invent new arguments and participate in public deliberation.[34] In analyzing higher education policy cases, I draw out arguments that frequently appear in debates about higher education, highlight how different arguments engage different types of audiences, and discuss what effects these arguments have had in different situations. Reviewing these arguments and learning how to recognize and critique or strengthen them will be valuable for leaders in higher education who want to learn to become public advocates for higher education. Thus, the book is concerned with helping an advocate's inventive efforts and group the relevant material, so that it can be easily found again when required. Ultimately, I argue that attending to these kinds of public arguments can be especially useful in three ways: (1) for defining value and forms of "accountability" to policymakers and other stakeholders; (2) for defending the public ends of education as a public good; and (3) for establishing deliberative processes in public forums about the future of higher education.

This book does *not* assume readers will have a background in higher education policy. At the same time, neither does it assume its readers are experts in the field of rhetoric. While you do not need to be an expert in higher education policy or rhetoric to be an effective higher education advocate, learning more about a rhetorical approach to policy can help make for better advocacy.

The Organization and Lessons of This Book

This book is organized around three rhetorical lessons for higher education leaders and policy advocates. Each lesson is drawn from the real-world case of the Spellings Commission, the thousands of responses it provoked, and its long-term policy effects, including the new measures of accountability that Spellings ushered into public higher education. The three lessons, I argue, constitute a way for higher education advocates to better engage policymakers, advocate for the public value of higher education in public forums, and create deliberative conditions for establishing public trust.

> Lesson 1: How to frame higher education as a public good, rather a private good, in policy discourse focused on accountability.
> Lesson 2: How to argue for higher education's value in democratic-centered, rather than market-centered, terms.
> Lesson 3: How to cultivate a style of policy leadership that prioritizes deliberative public engagement and cultivation of wise judgment, rather than metric fixation.[35]

In chapter 1, "The Spellings Commission and the Problem of Managerial Style," I introduce the Spellings Commission case study and show how conflict over the style of the Commission's report was thought to be at the heart of its failure to successfully engage higher education leaders. The chapter argues that the Spellings case exemplified a controversial style for higher education policy leadership, which I call "the managerial style." By analyzing key features of the managerial style, I show how this discourse style alienates most faculty and others in higher education from the policymaking process. I compare the managerial style with the academic style found in responses from many in higher education, and I argue that it is important for us to understand the effects of these different styles, especially the limitations of the managerial style for handling adaptive policy issues at the local and national level.

In chapter 2, "Rivaling Accountability," and chapter 3, "Building a Public Frame," I examine how those in higher education responded to policymakers' criticisms and calls for accountability. I identify and analyze common lines of argument (*topoi*) in public responses to the Spellings Commission. Specifically, I examine the rhetorical strategies and tactics that many in higher education used to rival the market-based accountability reforms proposed by the commission. For example, in chapter 2 I note how college presidents, faculty members, and professional associations argued against the commission's recommendations using five types of "dissociation" arguments, which consistently and effectively rivaled the report. Then in chapter 3, I show how advocates used what I call the "public frame" for higher education. The public frame is a rhetorical strategy advocates can use to provide an alternative to the market frame for US higher education. Use of the public frame in advocacy argumentation frequently includes one or more of four "public capacities," which exemplify the range of ways higher education's value consists of preparing students to contribute to the public good through developing their critical, ethical, technical, and deliberative capacities. Understanding the public frame and how its values are used as policy keywords is essential for advocates seeking to increase public support for higher education and build trust between higher education and the public.

In chapter 4, "Leading for the Public Good," I show how, following the Spellings Commission controversy, recent literature on higher education leadership and advocacy has trended toward either revolutionary and futurist or reformist models for reimagining higher education's purpose. I argue that, although some of these leadership models and alternative ideas for colleges have merit, most fail to commit to public or democratic aims. In contrast to these models, the chapter proposes a new model: the higher education leader as a public advocate. This type of leader can help institutions imagine a future for higher education that strengthens its public promise as a core mission.

In chapter 5, "A New Rhetoric for Higher Education Advocacy," I trace how the public arguments in the Spellings case have had a significant impact on current policy approaches to higher education today. Specifically, I consider the U.S. Department of Education's College Scorecard initiative, recent policy work by the Bill and Melinda Gates Foundation, and the bipartisan-sponsored College Transparency Act. I offer guidance grounded in lessons from the Spellings case about how those in higher education can learn from the commonplace arguments in this book to cultivate deliberative practice that can lead in policy efforts for the public good.

Last, some readers may be wondering whether these arguments for higher education can apply beyond the scope of accountability debates in the Spellings case to some of the more recent issues that put universities into political turmoil with their state governments (e.g., recent efforts in Texas and Florida to cut or limit DEI efforts at universities). While the scope of the book is limited to the debates about accountability and draws examples primarily from one case, I do think that the model of deliberative leadership that this book puts forward can help cultivate leaders who are more responsive to these public concerns. The book does not offer tactics for responding to these particular recent attacks on higher education, but it does offer some strategies and considerations for how to frame the value of higher education to policymakers, and it explains the communal rhetorical work necessary for ensuring that higher education is funded and supported as a public good.

1

THE SPELLINGS COMMISSION AND THE PROBLEM OF MANAGERIAL STYLE

To the extent that politics is an art, matters of style must be crucial to its practice.
—Robert Hariman

At a speech in Charlotte, North Carolina, in 2005, U.S. Secretary of Education Margaret Spellings announced her Commission on the Future of Higher Education. Her commission would join the legacy of other high-profile national education commissions under presidents like Harry S. Truman, whose 1946 commission produced the report *Higher Education for American Democracy*, or Ronald Reagan, whose 1982 commission produced *A Nation at Risk*. Spellings had just led the implementation of the No Child Left Behind (NCLB) education reforms in K–12. In an effort to extend her reform work to higher education, she introduced the context and rationale for creating the higher education commission: "In today's global economy, the best jobs go to the most skilled and most motivated workers." She warned, "In 1970, America produced more than 50 percent of the world's science and engineering doctorates. But if current trends continue, by 2010, we will produce only around 15 percent."[1]

At first, Spellings's argument for skilled STEM workers seemed to echo the nationalist fears of previous education reform agendas or acts, such as the National Defense Education Act of 1958, which positioned the United States as a country in crisis, falling behind other countries economically due to a lack of sufficient training in science, technology, engineering, and mathematics.[2] But Spellings's rationale for the Commission brought a new angle to the issue of the economy. Drawing from her personal experience as the parent of a college student, she explained:

> A few weeks ago, I dropped my oldest daughter off at college to begin her freshman year. . . . I found plenty of information on dining hall food, intramural sports, and campus architecture. I learned at one school that you can attend a Jimmy Buffet[t] Bash and a toga party all in one year. Who knew? . . . I didn't find much information on what courses to take, how long it takes the average student to graduate, and whether it's a better deal to graduate from a less-expensive state school in six years or a private school in four. I learned just how confusing the college process can be for parents. And I'm the secretary of education![3]

Spellings's remarks represented a turn from higher education reform efforts of other eras. Previous policy reports, such as the 1983 *A Nation at Risk*, had already set the stage for economic prosperity as *the* goal of US higher education.[4] But by aligning herself with parents of college students who were in need of finding the "better deal" and the means of managing the vast marketplace of higher education, Spellings suggested a *consumer rationale* for her new approach to higher education policymaking. While it appeared that she was appealing to parents and guardians of college-bound students, her speech that day served an important problem-setting function for the work of her higher education commission: she framed higher education as a consumer good and cast doubt on higher education's presumed value in its current form. Spellings invoked images of both a toga party and a Jimmy Buffett Bash, and portrayed institutions of higher education as lowbrow places of partying and socializing rather than places of expedient training at a good cost, offering an image of them as places that are chaotic, out of control, and in need of *better management*.

Indeed, Spellings's emphasis on the individual higher education consumer who requires means for managing the myriad marketplace options became the cornerstone of her Commission's reform approach and its subsequent recommendations in their final 2006 report, *A Test of Leadership: Charting the Future of U.S. Higher Education*. In perhaps its most controversial recommendation, the Commission called for a "consumer-friendly information database" for tracking and managing student progress, one that would also allow students and parents, as well as policymakers, to compare colleges and universities by cost, institutional performance, and student outcomes.[5] The proposed database offered a solution to the problem of how to determine "value"—if we could track information about students' progress through college, then we could compare them and know which colleges had more "value" than others. Such a database seemed like the best managerial solution to the many issues facing consumers and policymakers in a vast higher education marketplace.

Further signaling her managerial approach to higher education reform, Spellings selected a chairman from the business world for the Commission, Charles Miller. Miller was a prominent investment executive and the former chair of the University of Texas Board of Regents, appointed by George W. Bush. From that experience, Miller became known as the leader of the Texas K–12 education "accountability system." Spellings believed Miller would bring the managerial acumen needed in developing education reforms. As she argued in her 2005 speech, Miller was "a successful businessman, who understands what's needed to succeed in the twenty-first century."[6] In selecting Miller as chairman, Spellings showed that she was serious about using a managerial approach to reform higher education and solidified the association between success in business management and successful education policy.

But for many leaders in higher education, Charles Miller was a controversial choice. Historically, people with more experience in higher education teaching or administration had chaired presidential commissions on higher education. For example, the 1946 Truman Commission was chaired by George F. Zook, who served as president of the American Council on Education (ACE), and the 1982 Reagan Commission was chaired by David Pierpont Gardner, then president of the University of Utah. Of primary concern was that Miller had a reputation for taking an antagonistic stance toward higher education. As Kelly Field reported in her profile of Miller in the *Chronicle of Higher Education*, "[Miller] has never been afraid to take on the educational establishment, to be a thorn in the side of academe."[7] His background, specifically his family's "rags-to-riches" story, is cited in Field's article to account for Miller's matter-of-fact communication style:

> Mr. Miller traces his independent-mindedness to a childhood spent fending for himself. He grew up poor in Galveston, Tex., the middle child of a Russian immigrant father who ran a struggling grocery store, and a Brooklyn-born mother who died of Parkinson's disease before he graduated from high school. To help feed the family, he and his brother fished using improvised tools—a stick with a spike in it to spear flounder, a chunk of old meat tied to a string to catch crabs.

Six and a half days a week, before and after school, he worked in his father's store, buying produce and stocking shelves. "That's probably how I got my business techniques," he muses. "Learning how to mark a can of peas."

It was a difficult upbringing, and one he recounts somewhat reluctantly over dinner at an Italian restaurant near his Houston home.

"I don't look back on my past very much. I don't like doing it, and I don't think it's very constructive," he says. "I don't try to psychoanalyze myself."

He pauses. "I wish I'd learned to be smoother, nicer, a better communicator. I've had to learn people skills."[8]

The story of Miller's childhood and his confessed desire for better "people skills" highlights an important irony that unfolded throughout the Spellings Commission case: Miller's direct, sometimes antagonistic communication style was a core part of the public controversy—it influenced the tone of the commission's final report, it caused frustration for those in higher education, and it strained the relationship between institutions of higher education and federal policymakers.

From the start of the Spellings Commission, Miller made it clear that he had two goals: (1) to start a national "dialogue" about education, and (2) to give higher education a "wake up call" using "hard-hitting" language.[9] Though Miller was cautioned by colleagues that a "hard-hitting" approach might not be the best way to engage higher education leaders, he maintained it was the best way to get their attention; his strategy was to "jolt and shame, or roughly the educational equivalent of shock and awe."[10] According to Miller, something like a shock-and-awe strategy was necessary because when it comes to policy, "if you wrap it up in academic language, which is what the academy wants, you get long sentences and footnotes, and it gets put on the shelf. . . . Strong language gets attention."[11]

With Miller at the helm of the Commission, its final report was indeed written in strong language that got attention; it garnered thousands of national responses, receiving more documented attention than any government education commission in US higher education history.[12] The report sparked nationwide debates at colleges and universities, in academic media, and at regional policy forums between higher education lobbying groups and policymakers. Many in higher education were concerned by how the report characterized higher education as a failing industry, and how its policy recommendations focused on standardized accountability metrics. For example, in the opening to the report, higher education is cast in a negative light as "increasingly risk-averse, at times self-satisfied, and unduly expensive."[13]

The report also followed a familiar rhetorical trope of blame, frequently used in education policy reform efforts. As Mark Hlavacik argues in *Assigning Blame: A Rhetoric of Education Reform*, "the rhetoric of accountability serves the interest of legislators, removing responsibility for the success and failure of public education from lawmakers and placing it on educational professionals."[14] Specifically, the report attributed issues of access, affordability, quality, and accountability to higher education's own inadequacies ("squandered opportunities," "inefficient schedules") rather than accounting for the influence of other causal factors, such as the steady decline in public state funding for higher education for the last three decades.

A major point of contention in the public debate about the Spellings Report was the issue of *style*. As one anonymous participant conceded in a retrospective interview, "I do think . . . the language . . . can be a huge distraction from the content. . . . I feel like that's a significant lesson."[15] In separating "the language" from "the content" of the report, this participant echoed a separation that also became a rhetorical strategy in the Spellings case for shifting blame for the report's negative responses from the Commission members and Miller to the report's writer. For example, the report's writer was supposedly instructed, "Don't pull any punches in writing your draft."[16] It was later suggested that, despite Miller's previous calls for "shock and awe," if the professional writer had only *softened the style and tone* of the final report, then perhaps it would not have generated so much controversy.

Some in higher education tried to make clear that the report's style and content were not so easily separable. For example, in "The Flawed Metaphor of the Spellings Report," published in *Inside Higher Ed*, Daniel Chambliss argued that the guiding metaphors of the Commission's report—from business and manufacturing—created a problematic frame for the Commission's recommendations.[17] Similarly, Brian Huot argued that the report's reliance on business language distorted its sense of the true educational goals of higher education, thereby leading to recommendations and solutions that would actually be costly and ineffective.[18] In response, members of the Commission tried to distance themselves from the political fallout by shifting blame to the "style" of the report, rather than the "content" of their policy recommendations.[19] In doing so, they suggested that criticisms of the report from within higher education were superficial rather than worthy of serious consideration.

But how is it that the style of the report was viewed as both enormously powerful and important, yet also a superficial distraction from the policy recommendations?[20] The public controversy surrounding the Commission's report represents a key moment when the rhetorical style of a policy report became the focal point of contention—or at least *appeared* to be the main contention. Examining this paradox about style in the Spellings case is important for policymaking about higher education, since a major part of the controversy surrounding the Spellings Commission, and its "failure" to inspire higher education leaders, has been attributed to the style and tone of the report itself.[21]

I argue that at the heart of this policy controversy was a clash between two political styles, and therefore two corresponding sets of expectations for policy argument and decision-making: the *managerial style* (in this case exemplified by the leaders of the Spellings Commission) and the *academic style* (exemplified by many advocates in higher education). By using the term "style," I intend to draw attention to one of the traditional rhetorical canons that focuses on how word choice, selection of metaphors, and tone are inextricably tied to rhetorical effect in the process of public debate.[22] In particular, I argue that the Commission's use of business and manufacturing metaphors was far from superficial: it significantly impacted how the Commission interpreted higher education's problems and policy recommendations, and these metaphors became a key part of the debate itself. In this way, contrary to other studies of the case, the "style" of the report was not separable from the "content" of its policy recommendations in this case.

In what follows, I define the managerial style as a political style characterized by metaphors from the business world and their corresponding lexicons (e.g., "return on investment"), an emphasis on values of accountability, standardization, transparency, efficiency, and speed, and a prose style that is generally short and concise. It is guided philosophically by "metric fixation," or the belief that it is better to replace situated judgment and knowledge with quantifiable data, and that the best way to motivate people is by attaching rewards and penalties to measure their quantifiable performance.[23] The managerial style shares many characteristics of what Robert Hariman calls the "realist style," in that it often attempts to bypass deliberation through rational calculation and technocratic forms of information gathering to "discover," rather than collectively make or deliberate about, decisions.[24] The managerial style is what the realist style looks like under the influence of neoliberalism.[25]

In contrast to the managerial style is the academic style, which is characterized by metaphors of community and culture, values of democracy, civic duty, inquiry, history, and the slow process of learning.[26] It is guided philosophically by ideals of humanism and relies on a commitment to human capacities for interpretation and deliberation; in this way, the academic style shares many characteristics with what Hariman calls the "republican style," as inspired by the republicanism of the Roman orator Cicero, which focuses on a commitment to a shared public life.

Higher education leaders should understand for two reasons how conflicts between academic and managerial styles play out in a policy debate. First, these styles tend to shape stakeholders' expectations for how to engage in policy deliberation. Though the managerial style may be the reigning style among policymakers and even among some leaders in higher education today—and it may even have some merits—it has limitations and problems in the context of policy deliberation that are important to identify. Second, the issue of style is sometimes invoked as a reason to dismiss a policy recommendation outright; thus, style can become a way that people avoid or shut down deliberation about particular policies. If we are to undertake significant change, is important to understand how issues of style can inspire, shape, or stall public deliberation about education policy.

The Importance of Style

The styles we invoke when debating about higher education policy have important political implications. Styles of discourse produce emotional effects, help to create memories, and mediate our relationships with each other.[27] Focusing on style in public policy cases means paying attention to how the language used in policy licenses particular political actions and material effects. Put more simply, in politics as in life, how something is said matters.[28]

Of course, the managerial and academic styles are not exhaustive nor totally separate in practice, but they represent general starting places for categorizing types of discourse in higher education and their different structuring effects.[29] As a taxonomy, they should remind us that "political life is ineradicably a mixture of persuasive techniques, aesthetic norms, and political relationships working together in cohesive patterns of motivation activated through speech."[30] Essentially, the style of speech you encounter in higher education advocacy efforts can be understood as a key marker for helping to determine the effect of style on policy recommendations. The key questions to ask about it are, How does the style invite people to reason about higher education policy? And what does it encourage people to value in the process of deliberation and decision-making about higher education?

For example, attending to dominant rhetorical styles in the Spellings case can help us understand why many faculty in higher education—who expect the deliberative nature of the academic style when it comes to decision-making—were suspicious of the managerial style of chairman Charles Miller and the final report.[31] By contrast, when Miller claimed that his job as chairman was to tell higher education "the reality of the situation," he drew on aspects of a realist style of political discourse, dictating reality's terms to higher education leaders. The realist style, as Hariman defines it, is performed with frankness, straight-talking, or "truth-telling," which has itself become a successful trope in politics and policymaking, as well as in business and administrative contexts.[32]

A key characteristic of the managerial style relevant to policy cases in general is that it implicitly or explicitly denies having a style at all. To the contrary, it suggests that whatever the speaker says is therefore simpler (or less "academic"), and as a result truer and better. The performance of frankness in the realist style thus functions as a kind of antirhetorical rhetoric; it encourages people to distrust language as *mere* rhetoric, all while strengthening adherence to a particular style of doing politics.

The emphasis on style is relevant to the Spellings case because of how common it was to divide the style of policy discourse from its content in the ensuing debate about its recommendations. In retrospective interviews about the report's failure, the style of the report is regularly cited as a major source of public objections and resulting controversy.[33] But the disjunction of a policy into either its message *or* its style is a false one, which serves to shift issues of policy disagreement onto "mere style preferences" that get it in the way of the facts, rather than as elements that are fundamental to successfully implementing higher education policy in the first place.

Noticing how the managerial style of public policymaking responds to controversy by drawing a convenient cleavage between form (style) and content (policy) is important because it "radically separates power and textuality, constructing the political realm as a state of nature and the political actor as someone [who is] either rationally calculating vectors of interest and power or foolishly believing in . . . verbal illusions."[34] The managerial style's emphasis on market frames, its performance of directness and separation of style and content, and its antidemocratic ethos pose serious problems for the academic leader.[35] Negotiating the conflict between the academic and managerial political styles this poses perhaps the greatest rhetorical challenge to those who wish to shape higher education policy.

From a rhetorical perspective, style is not incidental, superficial, or supplementary: style names how ideas, values, and discursive practices are understood in communicative contexts.[36] Emerging from the communicative contexts of the business world, the managerial style of the Spellings Report arises from the foundational belief that all that is needed is an assessment of the problem, through gathering and collating information (data), listing options, calculating the costs of each, and acquiescing to the best course of action as preordained. Such a style in higher education policymaking attempts to remove or downplay the role of human deliberation with others from the process of policymaking in the first place by framing all problems as technical. The managerial style is problematic in policy contexts, since by its very definition policymaking is a "mediation of rhetorical and material forces" enacted by a community, not stoic resignation in the face of incontrovertible facts.[37] By contrast, the academic style I point to here assumes a different set of values: disciplinary expertise and experience in higher education, diplomacy, and an understanding of learning and the classroom. Most importantly, policy problems are treated as adaptive, cultural challenges that require a commitment to shared governance and deliberation.

It would be wrong to imagine that the near past of higher education policymaking in the United States was a perfectly deliberative state, abundant with political and economic potentials. The influence of managerial practices and ideals like New Public Management (NPM) and its historical antecedents has played a major role in the production of higher education culture today, especially since the 1980s. Indeed, the managerial style is quite common in academia, but it introduces a fundamentally different set of values than the academic style. What most public higher education advocates encounter today is not the incorporation of businesslike or managerial arrangements that previously seemed to possess subversive potentials for restructuring higher education as something outside its mainstream culture; rather, managerial style has become the dominant style for governance and policymaking.

The Managerial Style of the Spellings Report

The Spellings Report took a strident, "no-nonsense" tone and advocated for increased oversight of higher education through standardized metrics of accountability and a proposal for a national database of rankings. The committee's final report was criticized on numerous grounds, provoking a series of efforts from professional organizations and those within higher education to prevent the implementation of the report's recommendations.

To better understand how the issue of style and tone became so prominent in public debates about the report's policy recommendations, and to model potential critique of current and future policy debates, I examine three main points of contention found in public criticisms of the report in the following sections: (1) "market talk" (including market frames and business metaphors), (2) auditing and transparency (including demands for accountability and standardization), and (3) efficiency, transparency, and tropes of futurism (including criticisms of higher education as inefficient and slow to change).

Market Talk

Consistent with other education reform efforts in the later twentieth and twenty-first centuries, the Spellings Report stated that the aim of higher education should be *competition* in the global marketplace. For example, the report argues that "the need to produce a globally literate citizenry is critical to the nation's continued success in the global economy."[38] The report presumes that the end of higher education is the nation winning the global economy, and that market literacies for citizens are going to be the key to its success. The dominance of market ideals over all others in policy discourse generally is characterized by what Robert Asen calls "market talk." Market talk is any speech that extols the virtues of markets, competition, and efficiency at competing in them. As Asen explains, "in terms of its discursive style, market talk exhibits a realist pose that also serves idealist ends."[39] In summary, market talk promotes the ideal of the global marketplace by suggesting that it is indeed the reality in which higher education exists.[40]

It should not be surprising that the most recognizable aspect of the Spellings Report was its heavy reliance on metaphors and analogies to "the market."[41] Market metaphors and analogies serve two powerful functions in the Spellings Report: first, to cast the new "reality" for higher education as a rugged, competitive marketplace; and second, to define higher education problems and their solutions in terms of what the marketplace can already provide, assuming that education provides for the marketplace. In this way, metaphors of the market serve a "problem-setting" function in higher education policymaking, one where the same output is expected from every input.

In the report's preface, the policy problems for higher education are defined by a grim new reality. The report warns: "[The] world is becoming tougher, more competitive, less forgiving of wasted resources and squandered opportunities."[42] The report's emphasis on efficiency and waste is a key component of market talk rhetoric. Since the world is tougher and more competitive and "less forgiving of wasted resources," higher education should be equally tough and less forgiving of "waste," or of whatever lacks an easily recognizable use in relation to the market. Here, and in other higher education policy discourse, the use of phrases like "less forgiving" and "squandered opportunities" draws on the strict-father model of morality so common in American politics.[43]

A second function of market talk is that it limits the possibilities for policy solutions to business solutions grounded in business principles. These principles seek to make an array of complex social, cultural, and political problems in higher education translatable—and only resolvable—in market terms. The Spellings Report frequently compares higher education to business in the market to solidify this relationship: "American higher education has become what in the business world would be called a mature enterprise: increasingly risk-averse, at times self-satisfied, and unduly expensive. It is an enterprise that has yet to address the fundamental issues of how academic programs and institutions must be transformed to serve the changing educational needs of a knowledge economy."[44] Complex issues like access to higher education, or public funding for higher education, become problems with how educators understand (or fail to understand) the business world. This kind of policy discourse assumes that many educators cannot or will not comprehend how higher education has become a "mature enterprise" and must be transformed to better compete in the global marketplace of a needs-based knowledge economy. By mapping higher education onto a business and identifying the ways in which it is still *not* a business, the Spellings Report frames the problems of higher education as an imperfection with higher education itself—an "enterprise" with outmoded values and ideals.

In the Spellings Report, the marketplace is presented as totally immanent and totalizing, and historical perspective is totally elided. Explicit appeals to history (and there are very few to education history) are included only as a way to reinforce the continuity of policy aims and to emphasize the "universal" principles of the market and the grim fate of those in the past who have failed to embrace this law.[45] For example, the report invokes history to argue that higher education needs to respond with a better business model, otherwise it will fail like other failed industries: "History is littered with examples of industries that, at their peril, failed to respond to—or even notice—changes in the world around them, from railroads to steel manufacturers. Without serious self-examination and reform, institutions of higher education risk falling into the same trap, seeing their market share substantially reduced and their services characterized by obsolescence."[46] Here "history" is invoked in the report to serve as a warning or threat, but not to offer a critical perspective on the history of the problems that higher education currently faces. These kinds of appeals to history are characteristic of the realist style in policy discourse, which "teaches universal laws of power, not the value of local knowledge or different forms of power itself, . . . and it is invoked to inhibit argument rather than open the present to historical interpretation."[47] Such appeals to history perpetuate the assumption that there is a predetermined market truth to human history, which, when correctly divined, tells us how we ought to act in the present for the sake of the market's future. Market talk is thus about much more than strengthening adherence to market ideals; it is also a particular way of dehistoricizing our understanding of how higher education has been financed, what motivated previous reform efforts, and the relationships between federal government, state government, and individual institutions of higher education.

What is especially challenging about the prominence of market talk in the Spellings Report and subsequently is how it elides, or at least attempts to downplay, any other values besides its narrow definition of "results," as defined through market terms in business contexts. Its emphasis on results, defined in terms of profit and nonprofit, becomes a way for policymakers to sidestep concerns about corporate and commercial influence on the quality, quantity, or actual content of education, provided it gets results; it also promotes a general disregard for the public-versus-private distinction. For example, the report argues: "In this consumer-driven environment, students increasingly care little about the distinctions that sometimes preoccupy the academic establishment, from whether a college has for-profit or nonprofit status to whether its classes are offered online or in brick-and-mortar buildings. Instead, they care—as we do—about results."[48] This kind of thinking assumes that to care about such distinctions as the difference between for-profit and nonprofit, or the quality of online and face-to-face forms of education, is the outcome of higher education's inability to see the ends of education *like* a business. This is the managerial style at its most paradigmatic—at the same time that it avoids any appearance of self-interest, or values conflict, it devalues all other nonmarket discourses and "reduces all values to the use of values."[49] The emphasis on results (narrowly defined) thus lays the groundwork for managerial, commercial, and for-profit approaches to education, while denigrating the significance of public education in the United States. Most concerningly, the emphasis on results conceals the private interests that benefit from such a position.

Auditing and Transparency

One of the most controversial recommendations of the Spellings Commission was for the creation of a database to audit higher education outcomes. For example, the Commission argued: "We recommend a consumer-friendly information database on higher education with useful, reliable information on institutions, coupled with a search engine to enable students, parents, policymakers and others to weigh and rank comparative institutional performance."[50] From the perspective of most colleges and universities, this recommendation from Spellings suggested a bureaucratic nightmare and induced the fear that higher education would be reduced to the outcomes of testing scores or other standardized metrics. Concern about how No Child Left Behind (NCLB) reforms were implemented in K–12 education were frequently invoked by those in higher education.

By framing education policy in terms of managing technical problems, the report defined education policy solutions in purely technical terms. For example, so long as the policy problems with higher education are framed as a "lack of comparable information," then a database of easily quantified information seems to be logical, regardless of whether it will truly help to make better judgments. Such solutions rest on the assumption that increasing market exchanges requires systematized management to "store, transfer, analyze, and use massive databases to guide decisions in the global marketplace."[51] By relying on abstractions and vague, decontextualized statistics that stand in for the roles real people play in scientific, technological, and managerial systems, the report encouraged a technocratic form of decision-making.[52]

The impact of this emphasis on databases and audit structures distanced those in higher education from the actual process of policymaking. In the reality constructed by the Spellings Report, change in higher education depends on *compliance* tracked in databases. This approach to education has its roots in an antidemocratic ethos, one that sets up outside experts to manage education for educators.[53] It frames the issue of education achievement as one collecting information, rather than appealing to the situated expertise and wisdom of those in higher education to aid in defining solutions or judging quality.

As a policy solution, these databases tend to weaken trust in the qualitative judgment and situated expertise of faculty or administrative leaders. As Jerry Muller explains in *The Tyranny of Metrics*, "In a vicious circle, a lack of social trust leads to the apotheosis of metrics, and faith in metrics contributes to a declining reliance upon judgment."[54] From an actionable policy standpoint, the Spellings Commission's most prominent recommendation amounted to data collection—they assumed that building a database would be a good in and of itself. This is consistent within a logic of managerialism, but not necessarily a guarantee that its rationale will motivate people in higher education to make change.

Efficiency, Transparency, and Tropes of Futurism

The third component of the managerial style exemplified by the Spellings Report springs from the rhetorics of efficiency, transparency, and tropes of futurism to create a temporal sense of urgency. The Spellings Report emphasizes efficiency primarily in sections that focus on how to control costs through technology and online learning and sections that focus on how to assess student achievement. The report cites a study conducted by Carol Twigg and the National Center for Academic Transformation at Rensselaer Polytechnic Institute, which redesigned courses at the University of Massachusetts from traditional lecture formats to Web-based classrooms; the Spellings Report claims that University of Massachusetts students increased scores in biology by 20 percent and that the technology reduced costs for the student by 40 percent, concluding that "the results speak for themselves: more learning at a lower cost to the university."[55]

The combination of rhetorics of opportunity and progress both work to "create urgency, but they draw opposing conclusions about the nature of the moment, yielding on the one hand a rhetoric of opportunity or advantage and on the other a rhetoric of threat or disadvantage."[56] In this way technological discourse exploits the rhetorical concept of *kairos* in a way that is useful when analyzing contemporary education policy, where so much emphasis is placed on the promises of technology to provide education to more students, more effectively, and more quickly. Such claims often rely on metaphors of space and time as well as on "implied modes of technological and economic change to position technology, to argue for or against policy, to arouse fear and desire, to instigate action."[57]

To some extent, all policy discourse is oriented toward the future; it is "simultaneously descriptive and projective."[58] What is most significant about the use of urgency or timeliness in the Spellings case is its temporal metaphors. These metaphors include technical change characterized by metaphors of movement and speed. We are engaged in a "race" (to the top) or "accelerating" (to get to the future faster).

Even when the Spellings Report takes a descriptive stance, it is important to see these moments that describe our future as projective. For example, the report argues, "The future of our country's colleges and universities is threatened by global competitiveness pressures, powerful technological developments, restraints on public finance, and serious structural limitations that cry out for reform.... Our colleges and universities must become more transparent, faster to respond to rapidly changing circumstances and increasingly productive in order to deal effectively with the powerful forces of changes they now face."[59] This sense of inevitability is characteristic of the "futurology" of policy discourse.[60] It relies in large part on metaphors of speed and acceleration: the world is constantly changing, things are happening all around us, and they are happening fast. The emphasis on speed and acceleration is also prominent in the opening framing to the Spellings Report: "In tomorrow's world a nation's wealth will derive from its capacity to educate, attract, and retain citizens who are able to *work smarter and learn faster*—making educational achievement ever more important both for individuals and for society writ large" (emphasis mine).[61] In the global marketplace the report constructs, speed is essential for staying competitive against others in the global marketplace. This speed is not limited to student learning, though; everyone in higher education must work faster, teach faster, or assess faster to meet the demands of this new, real-time marketplace. As the report argues, "[Even] accreditors must continue and speed up their efforts toward transparency as this affects public ends."[62] The report's emphasis on transparency is a characteristic of audit culture, which extols transparency as an ideal that is presumed to be a panacea for governance issues, but this ideal is based on the fallacy of "the ideal of complete transparency"—that all knowledge can be transparent and known in the same way.[63]

If we consider the importance of speed, transparency, and efficiency for promoting the rhetoric of accountability, it should not be surprising that one of the Commission's findings is that "traditional academic calendars and schedules often result in inefficient use of an institution's physical plant and learning programs that are less than optimal."[64] Higher education's processes and its routines are framed as slow, tired, behind, outdated, and outmoded.[65] This image of higher education is a rhetorical construction that casts efficiency and speed as positive because they get us moving faster toward the future, but it is also a dark future; these constructions produce anxiety about such a future that is unknown and compels people to act in preparation for it by doing what they are told to do.

Blending the tropes of futurism and speed with the technocratic emphasis on efficiency and transparency, the Spellings Report creates a future reality in which the problems of higher education can only be addressed by changing all of its fundamental aspects: its aims, its daily operations, and its decision-making mechanisms.

The Academic Style

In response to the Spellings Report, many in higher education argued that the business metaphors and analogies in the Commission's report were not harmless stylistic flourishes—they were fundamental to a worldview and policy perspective incompatible with the aims of higher education. In an *Inside Higher Ed* article, for example, Daniel F. Chambliss argued that "education is nothing like business, especially not like manufacturing." Chambliss argued that the Commission's recommendations rest on assumptions drawn from the world of manufacturing *things*, which is evident in its lack of understanding how to educate *people*. "Coercion, it is believed [in the Spellings Report], is a simple and effective method for directing people. After all, if you put a steel girder on a flatcar, it will stay there until moved. And if you melt a steel girder to 4,000 degrees F., it almost never gets angry and storms out of the room or broods."[66] These concerns were also among higher education's inner circles and academic journals as well. Editor of the *Journal of Writing Assessment* Brian Huot published an article in *College English*, "Consistently Inconsistent: Business and the Spellings Commission Report," which argued that the report's emphasis on running higher education like a business was inconsistent with upholding accountability to a public good: "It seems inconsistent and shortsighted that a commission that largely advocates a business model for postsecondary education fails to understand that business forces are driving the very problems it laments. As institutions are less and less funded by the public sector, they are forced to recruit students aggressively, using market techniques that drive up the costs. A postsecondary system with generous public support would be able to focus more of its energies and resources toward instructional targets."[67] To make matters worse, according to Huot, the Spellings Report is inconsistent about its focus on market solutions. As the title of Huot's article makes clear, his main concern is the *inconsistency* of the report's policy arguments, which laud both democratic values and business values in ways that are incompatible. "Does anyone ask General Motors to contribute to the common good? Don't get me wrong; I support a strong social and democratic mission for higher education. But I can't see how that can happen when it is expected to be run like a business, nor can I understand the logic of projecting one model and expecting the performance of another."[68] The Spellings Report emphasized market-driven aspirations for higher education, as it simultaneously echoed references to previous eras of higher education policy that espoused more civic and democratic values. For critics in higher education, this inconsistency was indicative that members of the Spellings Commission did not have the expertise to be making policy about higher education: no one who understands what it means to educate people would be so misguided and unclear about the purpose of higher education. Indeed, Chambliss makes this argument at the end of his critique, pointing to how their report's logic fundamentally misunderstands human behavior and the nature of learning: "People set their own (often conflicting) goals; they resist coercion; they often surprise us. Admittedly, that makes working with them (healing them, leading them to salvation, encouraging their curiosity) a messy process. But I've seen no evidence that business people are better at it than educators."[69] Here, and throughout his article, Chambliss establishes that education is fundamentally about people and encouraging their curiosity, which cannot be mandated or coerced. He makes the case that the problem with the Spelling Report's recommendations is that they are all premised on a faulty view of higher education's purpose and primary activity.

This emphasis on the nature of learning as something that is messy or more complicated than a consumer transaction was echoed in a statement by the president of St. John's College, Chris Nelson. At a public roundtable with chairman Charles Miller and moderated by Doug Lederman of *Inside Higher Ed*, Nelson cautioned Miller and the Spellings Commission. In the style of an educator, Nelson argued that the language we use to talk about education matters. Subtly or not, we can all easily slip into market talk, and this language has more suasive power than we may realize:

> We should abandon the language of the marketplace. We are not delivery systems; students are not consumers; and education is not a product that can be bought and sold. The familiar metaphors of our commercial world come easily to all of us. For that reason alone, we should be wary of slipping into such talk; we may come to forget that learning is a cooperative activity, requiring commitment and effort on the part of the student, a far more complicated interaction than the purchase of goods at the shopping mall. Diplomas are not bought and sold; they are earned.

By reframing education as a "cooperative activity," Nelson emphasizes the humanistic and cooperative aspects of education, which is working together with others. Teaching is therefore not a "delivery system" with easy inputs and outputs that can be measured and tracked in the database, but a "complicated interaction" of people working together and developing relationships in the pursuit of inquiry and wisdom. What follows from Nelson's remarks, too, is a reframing of time and efficiency. He goes on to argue that since these are not the true aims of education, spending our time tracking and creating databases is actually a waste of time—it is *inefficient*. Learning takes time and can be measured only on a longer horizon.

By redefining the end purposes of higher education, Chambliss, Huot, and Nelson argue that the Spellings Report's recommendations fail even by its own espoused ideals of educational "quality" and "efficiency." Notably, these educators display teaching in their arguments, showing why business metaphors and analogies were not harmless, but were guiding the very logics used to create the policy agenda in a way that was inconsistent with our highest democratic values, which should guide higher education policymaking.

Managerial Versus Academic Style

At the core of the controversy over the Spellings Report and its policy recommendations was a conflict over two political styles (see table 1). The managerial style brings together the rhetoric of market talk, technocratic discourse, and tropes of futurism to create a discursive style characterized by the following features:

- *Market frames*: Metaphors and analogies that relate terms to business and that emphasize positive aspects of markets, competition, and efficiency.
- *Rhetorics of auditing and transparency*: Emphasis on data collection and transparency as key to ensuring quality of education. Characterized by abstraction, standardization of complex processes with databases.
- *Rhetorics of efficiency and tropes of futurism*: Future-oriented discourse and temporal metaphors of speed and acceleration. Emphasis on efficiency and inevitability of a technological future.

Table 1 Summary of key features of the managerial style

	Discursive form	Rhetorical function
Market frames	Metaphors and analogies that relate terms to business, industry, markets, and competition	To construct the global marketplace as a reality for audiences. To frame higher education's problems such that they require business or marketplace solutions
Rhetorics of audit and transparency	Abstraction, nominalization of complex processes with databases, including a relative lack of human agency	To reduce complex social policy issues to technical issues that can be resolved by experts and new forms of information technology. To shift authority away from the situated expertise of educators to data management companies or systems of data collection
Rhetorics of efficiency and tropes of futurism	Future-oriented discourse; temporal metaphors of speed and acceleration	To create a sense of urgency and to produce anxiety about the future. To create a system that necessitates technology as the efficient technical solution to social and economic problems

By contrast, the academic style (see table 2) attempts to strengthen adherence to democratic values of the public good and emphasize the university as a unique learning experience where inquiry, understanding, and the effort to learn in higher education contexts are most important.

- *Public frames*: Metaphors and analogies that relate terms to community, democracy, and citizenship.
- *Rhetorics of responsibility and duty*: Examples of educator's responsibility to classrooms, students, the public, and the active effort to learn.
- *Rhetorics of history*: Past-oriented discourse that focuses on historical precedent, tradition, and the importance of collective memory.

My goal in offering comparative examples of the managerial and academic styles (see table 3) is to illuminate how these styles can help us account for competing approaches to policy definition and deliberation.[70] When arguers

Table 2 Summary of key features of the academic style

	Discursive form	Rhetorical function
Public frames	Metapors and analogies that relate terms to community, democracy, and citizenship	To construct a democratic public sphere as a reality for audiences; to frame higher education's problems in terms of social and public consequences
Rhetorics of responsibility and duty	Examples of educator's responsibility to classrooms, students, learning, and a democratic public	To frame complex policy issues as social, collective problems, or adaptive challenges. To shift authority toward the situated knowledge of educators, students, and individual institutions of higher education
Rhetorics of history	Past-oriented discourse that focuses on historical precedent, tradition, and the importance of memory	To create a sense of purpose and gravitas; to emphasize how social and economic problems have emerged

Table 3 Comparison of guiding values for the managerial and academic styles

	Managerial style	Academic style
Guiding metaphor for higher education	University as a business	University as a learning experience
Aims	Operational efficiency; competition in a global marketplace; good return on investment	Inquiry, knowledge, and cultivation of public wisdom in a democracy
Knowledge	Quantifiable data	Qualitative judgment
Primary stakeholders to be accountable to	Institution, system of higher education; board and executive leadership, donors, accrediting agencies, and the Department of Education; private stakeholders and industry leaders	Students, colleagues, discipline
Decision-making	Hierarchical; real-time and data-driven	Horizontal; slow and deliberative
Relationship to time	Future-oriented	Past-oriented

approach policy issues using both of these styles, it can be difficult to have productive debate—or any kind of deliberation—since managerial and academic styles tend to stall out at early stages of policy deliberation, where questions of fact and definition need to be agreed upon.[71] For example, if arguers disagree about the fundamental purpose of higher education, or how to define its aims, it is difficult to deliberate policy decisions about how to improve its effectiveness, or even to agree upon the appropriate forms and forums for collective decision-making. Since both the academic and managerial styles are so common in debates about higher education, it is important for those who participate in shaping education policy to be attentive to the issues that can most inhibit productive and beneficent policymaking.

Rival Interpretations

In reflecting on the Spellings case, some readers may argue that there are competing interpretations of the cause and significance of these political styles. For example, it could be argued that this clash can be attributed to those in higher education—especially faculty—simply misunderstanding the *purpose and genre expectations* of public policy genres and reports: it is the job of policymakers to make sure that public funding for education is spent appropriately, so it stands to reason that their policy reports would be focused primarily on the business and accountability aspects of higher education. (I have sometimes heard this perspective raised by policymakers who are frustrated with efforts to make sense of higher education's resistance to the market concerns that higher education faces.) One problem with this interpretation is that the Commission's charge was much broader than this. It was supposed to provide a "vision for the future of higher education," not simply a cost-cutting plan. Even the stated goals of the Commission related to access, affordability, and quality of education involve social dimensions that are largely elided by the managerial style of the report.

Second, it could also be argued that those in higher education simply overreacted to a few of the statements in the report, which were really intended for a different *audience* of stakeholders. The style of the Spellings Report is not particularly unusual in the policy world—it is how people in policy and business write, and those in higher education should understand that they were not the only intended audience. However, the Spellings Report departed radically from previous presidential education commissions like the 1947 Truman Commission on Higher Education, which positioned higher education as a shared and necessary public good for democracy. Thus, the problem with this interpretation is that those in higher education were clearly part of the intended audience; Miller himself emphasized that he wanted to use language he knew was aggressive and controversial because he *wanted* to provoke a reaction from those in higher education. In titling the commission's aim as a "national dialogue," it signaled a collaborative give-and-take, but it became clear that this conversation metaphor revealed troubling—yet important—differences in how "conversation" plays out in the managerial style versus the academic style.

Third and finally, some have suggested that if the Commission had only *softened the tone*, they might have been more effective, that is, that even if it made the same recommendations, more people in higher education would have endorsed it. But the differences in tone and word choice between the managerial style of the Spellings Report and the academic style of some in higher education were not superficial, but discursive markers of deep philosophical issues about what it means to learn, to be human, and to educate others. They begin from different sets of common arguments and assumptions about the nature and purpose of higher education and, therefore, how to make policy about it. More significantly, the problem with the managerial style is not that it can be aggressive or hierarchical (though it often is), but that it typically does not value the slower process of deliberation about policy decisions as part of the decision-making process.

A Deliberative Style for Higher Education Policy

By starting with the issue style, my aim has been to show how managerial style not only introduces business metaphors or management language that may be incompatible with the educational values of many educators, but that it also limits the forms of deliberation that are practiced, the types of arguments that can be used in policy debate, and the possible policy solutions that can be attained.[72] In using the term "style," my goal is to highlight the fact that these ways of shaping policy are not predetermined in the Spellings controversy—styles of discourse can be taken up by whomever, in different situations and contexts. At the same time, style captures a powerful way that we indicate preferred or ideal modes of communicative engagement; in the Spellings case, what appeared to some to be a superficial debate about style came down to a fundamental disagreement about the primary purpose of higher education and the purpose of policy debates.

As a political style of policymaking and governance, the managerial style encourages us to treat complex education policy issues as *technical* issues, rather than *adaptive challenges*; in this way, it neither opens up possibilities for deliberation about the future of higher education nor inspires the collective action needed for major changes to important issues like access and affordability of quality higher education. Beneficent policymaking in higher education requires a compelling framing of shared problems (not blaming or scapegoating of individuals or groups), delegating responsibility appropriately, and identifying opportunities for action that can be accomplished by all stakeholders. Countering the negative effects of the managerial style thus requires attention to how our policy discourse either invites or prohibits deliberation about policy.

What is at stake here is not just a single report, but the cascading effects of a political style that has serious consequences for policymaking across higher education. While Margaret Spellings may not have achieved the federal legislation she hoped for at that time, her Commission and its report have been widely influential in putting higher education on the policy agenda for the first time in decades (see chapter 5).[73] More than fifteen years after the Spellings Commission concluded, we can see the impact of the controversy on efforts to change accreditation practices and the shift to an intensified audit culture of higher education, and most recently the College Transparency Act.[74] We also see this influence in hiring practices for college presidents, which increasingly focus on bringing business executives into higher education leadership roles.[75] In essence, arguments about the Spellings Report deserve study because its recommendations continue to be an influential part of a growing business and audit culture in higher education. Ultimately, and perhaps most importantly, the public arguments about the Commission's report set a contentious precedent about accountability and solidified a set of commonplace arguments that have shaped how institutions of higher education engage with policymakers today.

While those in higher education in 2006 blamed the Spellings Commission for being misguided, and while members of the Commission blamed higher education for being too defensive, this finger-pointing repeated a familiar trope of blame in education policy controversies; in other words, it is common for education policy reform measures to be motivated by attempts to shift blame to different individuals, sectors, or entities. Given the potential problems with blame in education policy, the Spellings case points to a need for repairing and cultivating public and faculty trust, which requires different forms of rhetorical reciprocity.[76] From this perspective, the most pernicious problem with the managerial style is that it tends to distance those in higher education from the policymaking process, especially faculty, thus straining the bonds of trust between policymakers and higher education. In the next chapter, I show how higher education advocates exemplified the academic style when they publicly rivaled the recommendations in the Spellings Report.

2

RIVALING ACCOUNTABILITY

Of course, what I want to say, and do say, is that the humanities matter. But as soon as we say that, we have to show what we mean by mattering, and that is where we get into a set of disagreements that are both difficult and invaluable.

—Judith Butler

In contemporary higher education, calls for accountability usually boil down to calls for schools to be held accountable to market values rather than to democratic values.[1] Scholars in rhetoric have tried to better understand how policymakers increased accountability rhetoric starting in the twentieth century. For example, one significant finding shows a transition from a "rhetoric of opportunity" in the early twentieth century to a "rhetoric of accountability" in the late twentieth and early twenty-first century, a transition that increasingly assigns blame to *educators* rather than other societal factors.[2] A second significant finding shows accountability policy proposals for higher education reform have been overwhelmingly bipartisan, across-the-aisle efforts that make them particularly difficult for higher education leadership to challenge.[3] After all, who could seriously argue that institutions that receive federal funding should not be "held accountable" to the public? Thus, for those working in higher education, the rhetoric of accountability poses a complex rhetorical problem in policy contexts: How can we rival or argue against such a seemingly positive ideal like "accountability" while upholding our responsibility and obligations to the public good and to our students?

To offer insight into this problem, this chapter offers an analysis of how many in higher education rivaled the accountability reforms proposed by the Spellings Commission, with the goal of providing real examples where those in higher education tried to uphold its public, democratic promise. Situated in a longer history of the rise of accountability rhetoric in higher education policy, the Spellings case offers important insight into the situated challenges of arguing against accountability measures that often take a great deal of teachers' time and energy but do little to improve the quality or affordability of higher education for students.

In what follows, I provide examples of how critics of these accountability measures used a rhetorical strategy called "dissociation," by which I refer to how people take a broad term like "accountability" and show that it contains a fundamental ambiguity or incompatibility of multiple terms in order to solve some policy problem. My review of the Spellings case identifies five types of accountability dissociations, each of which springs from the more fundamental idea that there must be different kinds of accountability. For example, marketplace accountability is often set in opposition to educational accountability.[4] This strategy of dissociation is not just incidental to accountability debates, though—it is the primary way that leaders must rival the homogenizing discourse of accountability today. Understanding how dissociation works can thus be a powerful way to bring clarity to policy cases. I conclude by arguing that higher education advocates can benefit from leveraging these strategies of dissociation to redefine accountability in education policy in an academic style, shifting its terms of accountability to *the public* rather than to *the marketplace*.

Accountability Rhetoric in the Spellings Case

In the findings to their controversial report, the Spellings Commission argued for a national, consumer-friendly database for tracking student progress with metrics that would permit student-consumers to compare colleges and universities by cost and outcomes, such as graduation rates and student debt.[5] At the time, the idea of an accountability database was easily the most controversial recommendation.[6] But more broadly, many leaders in higher education felt the commission did not engage them effectively in the policymaking process, while others thought it failed to develop a public, democratic vision for the ends of higher education. Instead of relying on appeals for the public good, it relied on a market rationale to create policy recommendations related to access, affordability, accountability, and quality.

While the Spellings Commission may have failed to implement the specific federal-level accountability measures it sought at the time, it succeeded in establishing a rhetoric of accountability in higher education that has accrued more velocity since the report was released.[7] One higher education representative summarized the consensus on "accountability" as a new key term for higher education in a retrospective interview: "The Spellings Commission opened our eyes to [the idea that] . . . more needs to be expected of higher education in the future [and . . . words like] accountability and building accountability architectures . . . are going to become part of the vernacular of higher education in the future."[8] As a result, the Commission prompted a series of efforts to create new assessment mechanisms for accreditation purposes, from the creation of Voluntary Systems of Accountability (VSA) to the College Scorecard. In short, higher education advocacy failed to alleviate the burden of doing assessment work for accountability purposes; however, its public advocacy efforts, in this case, solidified higher education's responsibility to do assessment work "voluntarily," and somewhat more so on their terms.[9]

The following section describes this rise of accountability rhetoric, beginning in the 1970s, leading up to the Spellings case in 2006; its history links the demand for accountability with current efforts to reform higher education.

The Rise of Accountability Rhetoric

As a policy keyword, "accountability" has been a standard in government sectors for quite some time, but its use in higher education is relatively recent. Richard Ohmann has traced the rise of accountability rhetoric in education to 1970. Before then, Ohmann found that only six articles in which the term "accountability" co-occurred with the term "education" in the databases at the library of the University of Amherst; however, from 1970–2000 the number of articles increased to 585.[10]

In a follow-up search at the University of Michigan library in 2009, Linda Adler-Kassner and Susanmarie Harrington found seven sources published before 1973 mentioning accountability and 5,817 thereafter. Narrowing the search specifically to "accountability and education," Adler-Kassner and Harrington found only two sources before 1970 and 750 thereafter (2010, 76). Both inquiries allow us to infer a distinct shift toward a rhetoric of accountability in articles concerning higher education occurring in the early 1970s.

As Ohmann observes about the historical moment of this shift, "It is no coincidence . . . that accountability emerged and gained strength as a coherent movement exactly when the postwar US economy was tearing at the seams, and when the right began to organize itself against sixties movements."[11] The rhetoric of accountability seems to increase following attempts to federally fund or widen access to public higher education.

The continued rise of accountability rhetoric in US education policy since then has likely had a significant part to play in the K–12 and higher education reforms that emerged in the early 1980s. The dominant education policy term through most of the twentieth century was "opportunity," as found in the Johnson-era reforms, specifically in the passage of the 1965 Elementary and Secondary Education Act.[12] One sees this shift from a rhetoric of opportunity in higher education policy discourse to a rhetoric of accountability more fully developed in the 1980s. For example, the rhetoric of accountability is already prominent at the federal level following the inauguration of Ronald Reagan, and Reagan's National Commission on Excellence in Education, which published *A Nation at Risk*, the first of a series of alarmist federal reports on education that continued throughout the decade.[13]

A Nation at Risk positioned higher education as the key to economic advantage for the United States in an increasingly global marketplace. As Holly McIntush has argued, *A Nation at Risk* fundamentally shifted the lexicon of education discourse from "education as a means of social and political equalization" to "education as a means to economic prosperity."[14] Positioned as an "aggregate resource" and "marketable commodity," education could then be divided into measurable units.[15] The results of using an economic or market frame and quantifiable measures included an emphasis on "accountability" and a managerial approach to accounting for quality and efficiency in higher education contexts. The term "accountability" thus became a "rhetorical frame" in the Reagan era, one that limited education policymaking to issues of measurable outcomes instead of a commitment to equality or equal opportunity.[16]

The shift from "opportunity" to "accountability" in the rhetoric of education policymaking also corresponds to a change in how education was funded, structured, and managed starting in the 1980s. As Asen has argued, whereas "'opportunity' justified a basic floor upon which students and schools could act, 'accountability' placed individuals at different levels of authority and prescribed a reporting system to transmit information up the hierarchy."[17] The belief in such a system represents a profound shift in public discourse and in social relations among individuals in higher education.

Two Paradigms of Accountability

The push for accountability in higher education that began to crystallize in the 1980s was accompanied by the development of new metrics with which to keep it accountable. Such measures were preceded by two basic "paradigms" of assessment, used for keeping education accountable up until then: (1) the "internal improvement" paradigm; (2) the external "accountability" paradigm. Both paradigms were first established for K–12 schools, yet they must be understood to appreciate the current tension concerning how colleges and universities *should* best be held accountable for academic outcomes.[18]

First, the "internal improvement paradigm" is largely focused on improving the institution itself through self-reflection, thus what it is accountable to is mainly internal to it. The "external improvement paradigm," on the other hand, is mainly external and cross-institutionally focused. The latter paradigm, where schools should be more accountable to external stakeholders and held in comparison with other institutions to improve through explicit, public-facing competition, began in the 1980s.[19] So, for example, whereas the controversies surrounding standardized testing in the 1980s helped to create an internal form of accountability or self-policing, the Spellings Commission called into question the quality of this type of assessment and pushed for an external accountability paradigm.

One reason the Spellings Report sparked the considerable controversy it did in higher education was that many educators and accreditation organizations were already deeply engaged in holding themselves accountable in internal assessment processes when the report admonished them for not doing so. Nevertheless, these processes seemed to be either elided or deemed inadequate. The Spellings Report strongly encouraged the second paradigm of assessment, one that, for example, could provide comparisons of student performance. During calls for increased accountability, Spellings and her commission appeared to ignore the expertise of educators who had already been internally assessing their work in higher education and holding themselves accountable for decades.

The Spellings Commission changed the policy landscape by shifting the audience for such metrics to the "broader public," which included student consumers and their parents or guardians, who wanted to compare educational outcomes and data across colleges to make informed investments. Identifying the paradigm shift in the authoritative body responsible for higher education assessment can help us understand why even the term "accountability" in the Spellings case provoked critical responses. Understanding this shift can also help make sense of the perception that those in higher education have an "aversion to transparency and accountability."[20] The backlash to Spellings was largely widespread opposition to a particular *form* of accountability, namely, a market-based approach to creating standardized metrics for comparing institutional data externally, especially data about students.

While the rhetoric of accountability has continued to dominate the policy agenda for higher education, the idea of being accountable, and for whose benefit, has been inconsistent. The discourse has shifted from a rhetoric of assessment (for internal improvement) to a rhetoric of accountability (for external comparison). The transition toward a rhetoric of external accountability helps us understand why critics of the Spellings Commission had to work so hard to create a publicly defensible position.

Dissociation as Advocacy Strategy

When policymakers call for accountability based on market terms that are incompatible with public or civic aims of higher education, what should we do? My review of the Spellings case suggests that advocates use a rhetorical technique called "dissociation." Dissociation is an argument technique that involves dividing a contested term like "education" into two terms.[21] In higher education policy discourse, a straightforward example of dissociation is found repeatedly in the rhetoric of liberal arts education. Advocates of the liberal arts often dissociate the seemingly unified concept of "education" into "utilitarian" (term 1) and "liberal" (term 2) forms of education, then advocate for the latter term.[22] The second term (e.g., liberal education) becomes a "criterion" used to assess the first term (e.g., utilitarian education). In the case of the dissociation of utilitarian/liberal education, proponents of liberal education typically describe liberal education as the best or truest form of education compared to the vocational aims of utilitarian training, which is only the *appearance* of being educated.

Similarly, the Spellings Commission report puts forth a modified reality for higher education in which a particular form of external standardized accountability is the only real means for ensuring the quality of higher education. Advocates who rivaled the report in higher education tended to rely on a strategy of dissociation to argue that the commission's market "reality" was only an "appearance" of quality. As Perelman and Olbrechts-Tyteca explain, "in argumentation, what one person terms appearance is generally what was reality to someone else."[23] In some instances, the separation between terms 1 and 2 also leads to a dichotomous dissociation that "is agonistic and consists of contested values that may be mutually exclusive."[24] Hence, the obverse of mutually exclusive dissociation is "pluralistic dissociation," which is "more ecumenical, assuming that contested values might coexist."[25] It is this pluralistic-type dissociation that David Frank argues is particularly important in policy cases: "As a methodological tool, the dissociation of concepts illustrates how dialectical pluralism can work to address concrete problems."[26] Dissociation is a particularly powerful strategy in policy cases where a plurality of stakes and perspectives are likely in play because it allows arguer to redefine dominant terms.[27] Thus, understanding how dissociation functions in highly politicized controversies like the Spellings case is also necessary for understanding how to account for competing perspectives present in a pluralistic society.

I call these dissociations "lines of argument" (*topoi*) for making cases in higher education policy to emphasize how those that persist in higher education debates can become the common argument topics from which additional arguments are created. Whereas Perelman and Olbrechts-Tyteca identified dissociations as the "residue of a dominant cultural tradition,"[28] and showed how groups of dissociations could characterize whole schemes of philosophical traditions, I argue that dissociations should be thought of as akin to familiar starting points for argumentation and "headings under which arguments can be classified."[29] In the following section, I explain how higher education advocates responded to policy arguments using five kinds of dissociations, or lines of argument, which higher education advocates can put to work when making the case for education as a public good.

Five *Topoi* to Rival Accountability

Responses to the Spellings Commission included at least five variations of dissociation in their arguments to rival the report's rhetoric of accountability. The five dissociations are notable because higher education arguers were trying to rival a discourse that was, in fact, not easily refutable. Calls for accountability are often tricky to oppose because serious persons in public positions of power cannot easily say, "I am not accountable" or "Higher education should not be accountable." The rhetorical challenge for the critic of accountability in higher education policy settings must be to convey a sense of commitment to the core shared value of accountability by dissociating the term into "educational accountability" (to students and their learning) and "market accountability" (to the global economic market).

In the Spellings Commission case, arguers had the difficulty of rivaling a call for accountability while also maintaining the democratic value of being accountable. Advocates had to go beyond the exigence of dissociating two types of accountability to create a series or fan of dissociations that spring from it, related to the mission, knowledge, assessment, authority, and motives for higher education.[30] In what follows, I define each of the dissociation types with representative examples. I focus on examples from college presidents, directors of major professional organizations, and college and university faculty members.

Singular/Plural Higher Education Missions

The main strategy for those in higher education was to argue against accountability by articulating the varying needs of different sectors of higher education and emphasizing their distinct missions. This dissociative argument challenges accountability rhetoric by emphasizing that there cannot be a single metric of accountability when there is a plurality of institutional mission types. The "institutional diversity" argument rests on a crucial dissociation between a singular system of higher education (appearance) and the plurality of institution types and needs (reality). In the larger corpus of responses, this dissociation was used most predominantly by higher education advocates in venues with audiences external to higher education, such as policymaking roundtables, or graduation speeches where students and parents or guardians were predisposed to being attentive to the value of a specific degree from a particular institution type.

Arguers used this *topos* to establish the uniqueness of each institution of higher education. For example, President Douglas C. Bennett of Earlham College argued, "The diversity of our institutions' missions and [of] our students calls for a diversity of measures, not some Washington-imposed single test."[31] Bennett's argument relies on a dissociation between a single (Washington-imposed) test and diverse evaluations of student outcomes.

Arguments like Bennett's "fanned" out, as other arguers subsequently used the "institutional diversity" argument to unpack how many different institutions serve the specific interests of dissimilar student types. For example, in her commencement address at Princeton University, President Shirley Tilghman argued:

> In a free-market system that has made U.S. higher education the envy of the world, students can choose between a large public research university like the University of Michigan and an intimate liberal arts college like Amherst College; between the science and engineering strengths of MIT and the performing arts reputation of Bard College; between The College of New Jersey to study to be a teacher or the Juilliard School to become a musician. Our system ensures that for each college-bound student, there is a college or university designed with his or her talents and interests in mind.[32]

Relying on appeals to "freedom," "choice," and "individual talents and interests," Tilghman advances a defense of higher education grounded in the values of the philosophical, liberal-free ideal of the liberal arts, albeit with a free-market emphasis.[33] By prioritizing the skills and interests of the individual over the global economy's interests, she also attempts to uphold the free-market ideal. Like Bennett, Tilghman simultaneously dissociates the presumed unified "system" or whole of higher education into the multiplicity of school types and missions. As a graduation commencement speech, her remarks are also a prime example of an *epideictic* or "maintenance" discourse, one that helps to strengthen an audience's adherence to a set of shared values about liberal education over time.[34] Tilghman's dissociations are a "values corrective" to the Spellings Commission that serves to strengthen adherence to the academy's traditional values of autonomy and freedom.

The tension between a unified or singular system and a pluralistic array of individual colleges was a key point of contention in the Spellings case. While the Commission sought to implement changes to the "higher education system," the concept of a single system of higher education, especially for those who work in higher education, was inconsistent with their lived experiences. As Ruben et al. concluded based on their interviews with higher education participants in the Spellings case, "there is little in their day-to-day activity that reinforces the sense that they are part of a much broader system." Faculty tend to work in separate departments and subspecialties, and different types of institutions operate independently, even within the same state or geographic region.[35]

Through the use of the singular/plural dissociation, such educators attempted to redefine public perceptions of the nature of US higher education, thereby setting the groundwork for arguing for different approaches to accountability and assessment than those proposed by Spellings. Notably, this dissociation was used most frequently by leaders at small liberal arts colleges (like Earlham) or private Ivy Leagues (like Princeton). One problem with this argumentative approach—as evident in Tilghman's speech—was that it sometimes relied on appeals to either a free-market ideology that privileged individual choice or to a "complexity argument," which amounted to saying "this issue is too complex for outsiders to understand."[36] While there is some truth to the complexity argument (few can understand the complexity of the higher education bureaucracy and its operations), in this case such arguments smacked of defensiveness and elitism and served to further divide "experts" of higher education from policymakers and the public.

Quantitative/Qualitative Forms of Knowledge

The second dissociation argument used by critics of accountability reforms argued that learning itself was too unique and contextualized to conform to a standard accountability metric. This dissociative argument separates the forms of "knowledge" presumed to be quantifiable for reporting metrics of accountability. Most often, the argument from those in higher education *against* quantitative measures of assessment is that many types of learning cannot be quantified because quantities cannot capture the qualitative dimensions of student learning. In the Spellings case, it was used largely in venues with audiences external to higher education.

This argument is similar to the one that different missions of different colleges posed a major problem for the development of a common standard. For example, President Christopher Nelson of St. John's College, Annapolis, argued that the accountability measures recommended by the commission—including a national database of student achievement data—relied on narrow and problematic assumptions about the nature of learning in its formulation for how to make accurate assessments of it. As president of a small liberal arts college and former president of the Annapolis Group of Liberal Arts Colleges, Nelson emerged in the Spellings case as a public spokesperson for the public benefits of higher education, specifically for the nation's liberal arts colleges.[37]

Nelson was asked to give remarks on the Spellings Report at a special forum of the think tank called "Ivory Tower Overhaul: How to Fix American Higher Ed," which was moderated by Doug Lederman of *Inside Higher Ed* and featured author of *Generation Debt* Anya Kamanetz, policy analyst for the Cato Institute Neal McKlusky, and chairman of the Spellings Commission Charles Miller. At the forum Nelson argued the following:

> Learning assessment ought to be an integral part of learning itself. It must be left to the classroom, the faculty, and the local institution. Nothing can be gained by broad, outside measuring instruments that cannot take account of what is going on between student and teacher, student and student, or the student and the books or equipment in the classroom. The report allows for such a solution but encourages the worst tendencies in us, [that is,] to teach what can be measured or to focus our attention on those things that are of least importance to living a thoughtful, examined life.[38]

Nelson dissociates "what can be measured" from "what contributes to a thoughtful and examined life," and decouples quantity from quality. Rather than reject the types of knowledge that "can be measured" outright, he establishes a hierarchy where what can be measured is of lesser importance than qualities that cannot.

For arguers like Nelson, the student measures the value of the learning experience, albeit with the occasional assistance of the teacher or tutor who helps the student in their endeavor. Therefore, learning assessment must be based on different criteria rather than only what can be gleaned from external testing or quantitative metrics. From his audience's perspective, Nelson's remarks suggest that the skepticism of external assessment is not about avoiding accountability for learning; instead, the proposed forms of assessment simply cannot measure what is most important and valuable about higher education.

The quantitative/qualitative dissociative strategy seen in Nelson's remarks is often used when defining learning as a process that unfolds in time, placing learning into the context of a whole life (as opposed to discrete, measurable units). For example, Tilghman argues that the type of learning one acquires in liberal education cannot be measured in the time frame offered by the Spellings Commission: "When it comes to the question of [knowing whether] . . . you are providing your students with a good education my answer is as follows: We can't really know until their 25th reunion because the real measure of a Princeton education is the manifold ways it is used by Princetonians after they leave the university."[39] Similarly, Nelson argues, "Earning a living (the object of utilitarian learning) is about means, and those means can be assessed and measured. Making a life worth living (the object of a liberal education) is about ends, and those ends are measured best by the quality of life lived over the full span of years—not so easy to assess by any general assessment instrument."[40] Tilghman's argument relies on the belief that "real" measures of learning *do* account for the way that time and lived human experiences impact the quality of education. By relying on a dissociation between means/ends, Nelson argues that a presumed unitary system of higher education, as well as its utilitarian focus in the Spellings Report, allows for an overly narrow focus on the means of a utilitarian education rather than the ends of a liberal education. For both Tilghman and Nelson, knowledge is gained through an individualized and contextualized human experience that only emerges over time. Learning cannot be measured and quantified in the ways prescribed by the Spellings Report with a consumer database of comparable education information.

The dissociations of apparent/real measures of learning and means/ends for higher education represent the clashing values of the liberal-free tradition and the demands of policymakers who expect a "return on their investment" from higher education. In these cases, arguers emphasized the way that only a qualitative approach to understanding the plurality of educational experiences has value. Such an emphasis springs from the "plurality" term in the singularity/plurality dissociation and from the quantitative/qualitative dissociation, which appealed to audiences of small liberal arts colleges and elite institutions, where their vision for education is one of a personalized approach to cultivating individual growth. Notably, the examples cited here were used in public venues (at a graduation commencement and a recorded public policy roundtable in Washington, DC) to appeal to those who were not educators themselves, but those who might benefit from such education (students, parents and guardians, policymakers).

Standardized/Progressive Assessment

The third dissociation argument used by critics of accountability reforms called the Commission's recommendations for standardization measures "too vague." This dissociative argument breaks apart the false unity of a "standardized assessment for accountability" and argues for multiple types of internal assessment instead of one. It attempts to resolve the incompatibility between "a desire for a standard metric" and a "desire for progressive education" (one that honors a plurality of students and abilities) to ensure a democratic and equal opportunity for education that may require a plurality of assessment types. The dissociation fans out from the previous one in that it assumes a dissociation of quantitative/qualitative, but unlike the quantitative/qualitative dissociation, it appeals more to insiders in higher education, who are already familiar with assessment and accountability demands but less familiar with the myriad forms it might take.

Rather than try to challenge the aims of accountability and issues with assessment altogether, educators argued that Spellings did not account for the wide variety of possible forms of assessment that can be used to create common standards. In this case, "assessment standards" were dissociated by critics into two forms: bad ("NCLB-style") and good ("progressive"). This argument was advanced more frequently by representatives from state and community colleges and appeared in internal correspondence among academia's professional organizations, where educators had public space to negotiate the terms of assessment that seemed most appropriate.

This perspective of compromise was exemplified in a response from Gerald Graff, former president of the Modern Language Association (MLA), and Cathy Birkenstein in their article "A Progressive Case for Educational Standardization: How Not to Respond to the Spellings Report."[41] They argued, "The wholesale rejection of common standards fails to distinguish between good and bad forms of standardization."[42] Relying on a dissociation between "NCLB-style standardization" (bad) and "progressive standardization" (good), they argued the following: "Engaging in this standardization process is important, we think, not just because without it No Child Left Behind–style versions of standardization may be imposed on us unwillingly, but because intelligent standardization is critical to our mission of democratic education, which entails being as explicit as possible about the essential moves of academic and public-sphere literacy and helping as many students as we can to master them. In our view, higher education does need common standards, even if the Spellings Commission says it does."[43] Graff and Birkenstein were not alone in their emphasis on an "intelligent" form of standardization, especially if it could foster the kind of democratic reforms that had historically widened access to higher education. Their response differs from other critics of the Spellings Report in that they anticipated—and tried to prevent—an overemphasis on higher education "autonomy" and anti–federal government sentiment, which has been characteristic of debates in US higher education policy history.[44] Their "progressive case" attempts to highlight the democratic potential in standardization efforts, relying more on the ideals of the *artes liberales* tradition than the liberal-free tradition of the liberal arts; that is, they relied on the ideals of a shared culture and higher education's demystifying potential to help prepare students for participation in a democratic culture.[45]

Graff and Birkenstein's dissociative strategies adhere to the discourse of standardization rather than reject it outright. Critics using this strategy affirmed their commitment to accountability measures while also redefining the term, a vital characteristic of the dissociative strategy in general. As

Schiappa has argued, "Dissociation can be used to suggest that a new definition is not a threatening break from tradition; thus, it is a particularly powerful tool to use to maintain a given lexicon while changing its referents."[46] For advocates like Graff and Birkenstein, it is important to reclaim the discourse of standardization—especially for its "democratic potential"—rather than reject it. The standard/progressive dissociation was widely circulated among other academics in the humanities, presumably because it represented a compromising position that still positioned educators as authorities for handling assessment and accountability reforms. This argument appealed to audiences of state colleges and universities already accustomed to various forms of assessment reforms and proposals for the sake of accountability to state and local government.

External/Internal Authority

The fourth dissociation argument used by critics of accountability directly questioned the ability or authority of those outside the classroom to assess student learning. This argument attempts to resolve the incompatibility between the way education and learning are both personally enriching experiences for students who seek to know themselves and flourish and also experiences that must be judged externally by parents or guardians, employers, and policymakers. This dissociation was used to appeal to both insiders and outsiders in slightly different venues. For example, when used to appeal to outsiders, it served as a way for educators in higher education to establish their authority and demarcate their expertise to judge. When used to appeal to insiders, it served to reinforce values already shared by many in higher education, reminding educators that they have the authority to push back against outside calls for accountability since they are the experts.

The external/internal dissociation was prominent in the example from Nelson, who remarked, "Nothing can be gained by broad, outside measuring instruments that cannot take account of what is going on between student and teacher, student and student, or the student and the books or equipment in the classroom."[47] As part of an effort to refute the ability of standardized accountability measures to capture the qualitative dimensions of learning, Nelson also relies on the dissociation of outside/inside or external/internal. A variant of Nelson's strategy appears in a response from Linda Adler-Kassner, then vice president of the Council for Writing Program Administrators, and Susanmarie Harrington, who argued the following: "Accountability gives power to a select few—those who are designing and overseeing the assessment designed to demonstrate accountability. In the process, it is likely that this frame also removes authority from those on the ground—teachers, probably, and certainly students. There is a whiff of doing and being done to here, rather than a sense of shared or collective action."[48] Adler-Kassner and Harrington foreground the problem of how assessment design alters participants' stakes in education and their role in the constructed value hierarchy of higher education. By dissociating key constituencies into "those who are designing and overseeing the assessment" from "those on the ground," Adler-Kassner and Harrington draw attention to the different positionalities and forms of authority constructed by calls for accountability. Their dissociation of constituencies into designer/designed brings about "profound change" in considering accountability metrics because it encourages us to reflect on the external/internal pair. While accountability involves "proving" whether something is effective or not, a good assessment for this camp focuses on "improving."

Dissociating external from internal accountability assessors creates a philosophical pair concerned not merely with statuses but, fundamentally, with forms of expertise. While some in higher education were divided about whether and how to develop assessment metrics, almost all agreed the work should only be conducted by those internal to higher education. By positioning the Spellings Commission and other policymakers as outsiders whose designs might do more harm than good, this dissociative strategy demarcated teacher expertise in classrooms and on campus. This was also the most widely used dissociation for appealing to both insiders and outsiders in somewhat different venues. When used to appeal to outsiders, it served as a way for educators in higher education to establish their authority and demarcate their expertise. When used to appeal to insiders—as in the case of Alder-Kassner and Harrington—it served an epideictic function, reminding educators that they have the authority to push back against outside calls for accountability.[49]

Profit/Pure Motives

The fifth dissociation argument commonly used against accountability focused on the interests of those who would conduct such assessments to raise suspicions about commercial interests in assessment metrics, rankings, and the commission's proposal to create a student record database. The profit/pure motives dissociative argument bifurcates pure and profit-driven interests and is often used by those in higher education to appeal equally to both insiders and outsiders and establish insiders as more trustworthy when it comes to assessment practices. When used on insiders in higher education, it was generally employed in external venues with wide internal circulation such as the *Chronicle of Higher Education*, *Inside Higher Ed*, or scholarly manifestos published by academic presses.

The profit/pure motives dissociation is evident in an *Inside Higher Ed* article by Emily Toth, a Robert Penn Warren Professor of English and Women's Studies at Louisiana State University, who warned: "The commercial ranking services, once delivered this treasure trove of numbers that bear the imprimatur of regulatory agencies, will construct increasingly convoluted and methodologically flawed rankings, cloaked with regulatory authority, conveniently forgetting the caveats about data contained in obscure footnotes in the government reports."[50] Similarly, in the presidential address at the Council of the Colleges of Arts and Sciences at the annual meeting in November 2008, Matthew C. Moen argued: "Accountability is also troublesome to the extent it has become a cottage industry. Assessment academies, publishers, the touring and testing companies, EduMetry, OWL Software, Insight . . . they all stand to benefit from pervasive testing. Consultants are likewise riding this wave of policymaking to lucrative arrangements."[51] In raising suspicions about the motives of those demanding accountability, the motives of persons true to higher education are defined as "pure" and therefore preferable to the "profit" motives of those who only appear to work in higher education.

Finally, while many critics of the report were concerned about the for-profit interests of the data management industry, a related concern for many was the privacy of student information. Robert Berdahl, former president of the Association of American Universities (AAU), remarked: "While AAU is undertaking the development of information about the graduates of its institutions, we have concerns about issues of privacy that would arise with the creation of an extensive federal database containing all student records. Such a central repository would be contrary in letter and spirit to current student privacy laws. There are legitimate concerns about how such records could easily be abused by authorities seeking information for purposes other than those of education."[52] The AAU response attempted to cast doubt on the need and reliability of the information gathered through the proposed accountability measures by relying on dissociation between corrupt profit-driven motives and those deemed pure or authentic. Arguers aligned the pure motives of those in education with student privacy, thereby separating them from those who would abuse student information for impure (e.g., profit-driven) motives.[53] This dissociation—perhaps more than all others—is most characteristic of the divide between those working directly in higher education and those directly involved in the business sector who served on the Spellings Commission.

The Implications of Dissociation Arguments

Using the technique of dissociation, leaders in higher education mounted a strong case against the Spellings Commission's recommendations for increased external accountability. Most notably, these critics helped stop efforts to turn the Commission's recommendations into federal legislation through public and professional advocacy work. Their efforts were significant because they prevented an official transition of power from regional accrediting agencies to the Department of Education. This outcome took a concerted effort and demonstrates one way those in higher education are capable of challenging and shaping accountability policy rhetoric through consistent and continuous advocacy work. That said, by using these dissociations—specifically the external/internal—higher education advocates shifted the responsibility for accountability efforts back onto higher education institutions. In doing so, they reclaimed authority for conducting their own assessment, but did not succeed in substantially changing the public rhetoric of higher education policy toward more public aims.

In reviewing the most common dissociative arguments in this case, key differences were found in the audiences addressed by each type and the venues in which they were used. For example, the dissociative *topoi* singularity/plurality, quantitative/qualitative, and profit/pure were leveraged more frequently by advocates from liberal arts colleges, elite research universities, and the professional organizations of research institutions like the Association of American Universities (AAU). For these advocates, external accountability in the Spellings Commission's final report was made to seem as if it violated the fundamental values of freedom in education, including freedom of inquiry and freedom *from* a single standard. By prioritizing individual autonomy and the qualitative aspects that make institutions and individual learners unique, arguers emphasized values their audiences were predisposed to, and that ought never to be guided by profit-making motives.

Notably, these three dissociations were often employed in venues to audiences "external" to higher education; that is, they were used to help policymakers, students, parents or guardians, and other stakeholders who might not understand the varied landscape of higher education institutions. The singularity/plurality dissociation was also key for advocates here. However, one danger of using this argument is how it can lead to, or be conflated with, the "complexity argument," or a kind of accountability relativism. Those perceived to be accountability relativists claim there is too much complexity to be captured by common standards or any similar forms of assessment because there is a diverse set of missions. One problem is that some arguments that used this strategy failed to distinguish "good" and "bad" forms of testable standards, consigning them to the waste bin.[54] Other critics of accountability relativists, such as state policy director Travis Reindl, warned in the context of policy strategy that "the gas mileage we're getting out the complexity argument is about to run out."[55] Finally, there were advocates who argued that teacher-researchers should reframe accountability in terms of "responsibility" for assessment.[56] In summary, critics of accountability relativism argued that it was politically strategic at the time to redefine the terms of accountability rather than reject it outright.

The standard/progressive and external/internal dissociations were favored by arguers from regional state schools and community colleges, presumably because they were more accustomed to being held accountable to external stakeholders such as state and local taxpayers. These arguments were also used in venues inside of higher education among fellow educators. For example, organizations representing state colleges were less concerned about whether external forms of accountability would be expected and more concerned about figuring out the best way to conduct assessments ethically and how to report their assessment information publicly. Graff and Birkenstein's "progressive argument" for standardization seemed to be the best compromise—and arguably the most effective in this case—but it had two consequences that arguers should be aware of.[57] The first consequence was that their position seemed to invite efforts for *more* metrics of accountability. Indeed, some higher education advocates proposed a plethora of voluntary and self-imposed forms of accountability to maintain autonomy and avoid relinquishing control to the Department of Education. The second consequence was that framing their position on assessment as one of "intelligent" versus "unintelligent" standardization perpetuated perceptions of elitism that frustrated some policymakers.

Although advocates in higher education helped prevent the Spellings Commission's accountability measures from becoming federal legislation, some uses of this strategy reveal troubling implications that advocates should be aware of before using it. Perhaps most notably, arguers using the external/internal authority dissociation tended to reinforce a general suspicion of government involvement in assessing higher education, which was supported by values of freedom and individual autonomy. A growing concern about government meddling may have seemed reasonable at the Spellings Commission's time, particularly given the context of No Child Left Behind. However, as we have seen over the last decade, an apathetic or antagonistic relationship between higher education and policymakers poses a worrisome threat to public support of higher education. We need productive ways of discussing policy issues that consider higher education's public aims and ensure that the best aspects of higher education are not diminished or thwarted in attempts to demonstrate market accountability.

Value in Education Today

Public debates about higher education accountability are far from over, as evidenced by the launch of the Bill and Melinda Gates Foundation's Postsecondary Value Commission in 2019, which focuses on assessing the economic benefits of a college education (see chapter 5). While the commission's website names civic participation and equity as core values, and it has done more to focus on a diversity of mission types, including HBCUs, its policy efforts are filtered through a rhetorical framing that prioritizes individual economic gains over shared public concerns. Rather than defensively forestall these efforts, higher education advocates could use dissociation to help encourage the commission to reprioritize the values guiding their work.

Advocates could use the market/public dissociation to help prioritize the value of *public accountability* over *market accountability*. To further align values of public accountability, advocates could use the profit/pure dissociation to help prioritize cooperative inquiry over competitive performance as the primary motive for higher education. Or advocates could use the quantitative/qualitative dissociation to help prioritize qualitative data about students' learning experiences over quantitative data about degree attainment. The specific application of the arguments will change by situation and audience, but used as an inventive heuristic, these dissociations can help advocates create a reality where shared public goods are prioritized over private economic ones in higher education policy.

In the next chapter, I offer examples of how advocates in higher education attempted to rival the Spellings Commission's market vision for higher education using a rhetorical strategy that I call "the public frame." I argue that the public frame is a broad and adaptable strategy for shifting the grounds of argumentation away from a narrow market framing for higher education and toward a more expansive sense of higher education's public promise.

3

BUILDING A PUBLIC FRAME

If today's universities are to build successful relationships with those publics—if they are to be understood as genuinely providing a public good—we must not only argue for but also model what understanding our work as a public good means.
—Kathleen Fitzpatrick

How can we make a strong case for higher education as a *public good*? Or, to raise a question from Kathleen Fitzpatrick in *Generous Thinking*: "How might we communicate the socially oriented, nonmarket value that higher education produces?"[1] Drawing representative examples from prominent public academics, the president of a small liberal arts college, and responses from academic professional organizations, this chapter presents a second set of common lines of argument (*topoi*) that have been used to advocate for the range of ways that US higher education serves the public good. These arguments are representative of four "public capacities" that higher education helps people to cultivate, capacities that are central to a democratic way of life: (1) critical, (2) ethical, (3) technical, and (4) deliberative.

Whereas chapter 1 established style as a key part of the policy process, and chapter 2 offered common dissociation arguments as a way to resolve value disagreements, this chapter offers a broader rhetorical strategy for uniting those in higher education in a common purpose: *the public frame*. The public frame offers a set of four arguments that can be used in a variety of policy situations for a variety of audiences. For readers who are scholars of rhetoric and public sphere theory, this chapter also offers a vivid example of how our public values for higher education are brought into being and strengthened through public debate. While the arguments highlighted in this chapter may seem most familiar to those in the humanities, these arguments also appeal to a wider range of readers by showing how they can be used to advocate for the public value of higher education more generally.

Our Public Failure

In the surge of literature about the public "crisis" of higher education today are scholars and activists who point out that it has been higher education's *failure* to make a strong case for how education serves the public good that accounts for the troubled state of higher education today. For example, in Christopher Newfield's 2016 book *The Great Mistake*, he argues that public university managers failed to "make the strong case for [higher education's] social, non-market, and indirect benefits."[2] Similarly, in "The Undeserving Professor: Neoliberalism and the Reinvention of Higher Education," Luke Winslow observes that it is faculty in higher education who "failed to provide cogent alternative language to market-conducive versions of higher education."[3] Winslow and Newfield's arguments are echoed by others who call for greater public advocacy for higher education, specifically the need to articulate the significance of higher education in terms of its collective, public ends beyond job training or other market-driven aims.

While many seem to be in agreement that a failure to make a stronger public case is to blame, what remains unresolved is *why* those in higher education "failed" to advocate for funding higher education as a public good. Why didn't faculty and university leaders make the public case for higher education when public funding started declining? Were they ignorant about how to do it? Were they unable to anticipate the long-term effects of allowing a market discourse to dominate public debate? Is the failure to make the public case, as Newfield argues, a kind of "willful blindness," suggesting they did know but were unwilling to do it? Or perhaps is it the case that helping others to value higher education as a public good requires something more than just a new "messaging" campaign?

This chapter assumes that making the public case for higher education and creating a "publicly responsive infrastructure" is a complex *rhetorical* challenge that involves the discovery and creation of shared values in ways that call a public into being.[4] The shared, public work of rhetoric is thus an "adaptive challenge,"[5] one that requires (1) cultivating space in our academic lives for deliberating about our values; (2) struggling with our own often-contradictory desires and hopes for higher education; and (3) having opportunities to develop and test out alternative discourses that "make us wonder about what we are doing."[6] This challenge is distinctly rhetorical insofar as it is a challenge that requires making responsive arguments to others, in the right places, at the right times.

I argue that we might begin the process of inventing a "publicly responsive infrastructure" by first inquiring into how those in higher education have previously engaged in public advocacy work—or failed to engage—and why. In what follows, I analyze how leaders in higher education, especially in the humanities, were successful in mobilizing responses to the report by providing a rhetorical strategy I call the "public frame" for higher education to rival the market frame used in the Spellings Report.

The Challenge of Defining Higher Education as a Public Good

There are many paradoxes in higher education's public promise. Can we say in good faith that higher education is a public good when it clearly has so many private benefits? Some historical perspective may be useful here in sorting out our imprecise definitions. As education historian David Labaree explains in his book *A Perfect Mess*, our inability to pin down a singular mission or purpose for US higher education actually correlates with its strength as a world-renowned enterprise that has been able to offer a lot of different things to a lot of different types of people in its relatively short history (when compared with European counterparts). He explains how US higher education is at once "the people's college, the party school, the scholar's retreat, the economic engine, the public park, the tower of learning, the training ground, the bulwark of privilege, the cultural repository, the public entertainer, the gateway to the middle class, the club, the colosseum, and the conservatory.... It's an organized anarchy, a perfect mess."[7] Many critics of and within higher education have pointed to the major problem in policy as a shift in its defining characteristic as a public good. Scholars often take as a starting point the Higher Education Act (HEA) of 1965—the "golden age" of higher education—and then interpret "the fall" of higher education since that era.[8] As Jeffrey Williams argues, the funding model of higher education, cuts to state funding, and the increase in student loan debt have structurally transformed higher education from a public good to a private good. Put simply, higher education is perceived to be a private good insofar as it provides benefits to individuals, and it is perceived to be a public good insofar as it provides benefits to everyone in a given society (whether they attend college or not).[9]

In *The Great Mistake*, Newfield makes a strong case for the need to define higher education as a public good that is a *social good*. In contrast to economic definitions of the public good, Newfield advocates a *social* definition of the public good as "a good whose benefit continues to increase as it approaches universal access."[10] The more people have access to it, the greater the social benefit. But higher education as a social good takes place in "a rivalrous economy." As he goes on to explain by applying it to higher education: "Public higher education is a public good, and yet it has the features (rivalrous and excludable) of a private good." This definition leads Newfield to propose instead that higher education, especially in the United States, is a "dual good" or "double good," insofar as it has *both* private and public impacts. His point is that our public rhetoric extols mostly the private benefits of higher education because those benefits are most easily understood by parents and students and since it seems easier to quantify the private value in terms of income. Like Newfield and Labaree, this chapter assumes that US higher education is—in some sense—*both* a private and a public good. And this applies not only to the institutions defined as public, but also to private institutions as well.

One way that we might move beyond debates about whether higher education "really is" a public or private good is to focus on what is at stake in our definitions of higher education. By focusing on what's at stake, we move into the realm of the rhetorical. As Edward Schiappa argues: "Our inability over the centuries to agree on definitions that identify the essence or nature of a phenomenon is less a failure to follow some correct methodology than a reflection of our variable needs and interests."[11] A rhetorical approach to policy definition focuses on our variable needs and interests and the way that our definitions of things like "public good" are not simply facts, but situated *choices*. The language that we choose to use involves a series of choices—intentional or not—that we need to become aware of and navigate more carefully. For example, public sphere theorists have long argued that the private/public distinction matters to the extent that how we define whether something is public or private creates the conditions under which we do something about the issue.[12] So defining higher education as a public good is a necessary rhetorical precursor to doing something collectively about the problem.

My point is that our inability to discuss higher education's public value is often troubled by a lack of common arguments for talking about what should constitute a public good; in essence, our inability to articulate the public value of higher education speaks more to the paucity of our public rhetoric for what a vibrant, democratic public sphere can and should be. I advocate that we should build a rhetorical "frame" for higher education as a public good, one that brings into focus civic values and social benefits. I am interested in building that public frame and using it in a variety of situations to help bring aspects of higher education's public significance into focus.[13]

This approach to talking about public values is guided by the work of Belgian argumentation theorists Chaïm Perelman and Lucie Olbrechts-Tyteca in *The New Rhetoric*, who are concerned with helping people to reason about their values.[14] Rather than assuming that people disagree in a policy debate because they hold different values, they argue instead that people tend to hold the same values but disagree in particular cases when they *prioritize* those values differently. To explain this phenomenon, they offer the useful concept of "value hierarchies"—or the way that people hold multiple values simultaneously in different ranks of priority.[15] One way of making sense of this in the case of higher education is to say that most of us hold public *and* private ideals for higher education, but we prioritize these ideals at different times.

What Perelman and Olbrechts-Tyteca's theory of value hierarchies offers is a way of looking at policy arguments as the opportunity to co-construct and reconsider our hierarchies of values. In the case of higher education policy, we might do well to see our task not as convincing constituents that higher education *really* is a public good instead of a private one, but about helping them to see why it is important to prioritize the public benefits over the personal benefits. The public frame that I define in this chapter is one strategy for helping to shift people's value hierarchies for higher education such that public values are prioritized.

The Public Frame in the Spellings Case

Following the release of the first draft of the Spellings Report in 2006, leaders in higher education, especially in the arts and humanities, responded quickly, circulating responses in the *Chronicle of Higher Education*, in professional organization newsletters, and in speeches on college campuses. The Association of American Colleges and Universities (AAC&U), for example, denounced the Spellings Report's narrow framing of the goals of higher education: "The longstanding and distinctively American goal of preparing students for engaged citizenship is ignored entirely by the [Spellings] Commission. In this regard, the complete failure even to mention the importance of history, culture, the humanities, the arts, or to highlight the growing service-learning movement shows a dramatically downsized conception of college learning."[16] Similarly, David Breneman, dean of the Curry School of

Education at the University of Virginia, criticized the report on the grounds that "[the Spellings Report] slights the non-economic, social benefits that we used to associate with higher education, including the cultivation of ethical and aesthetic capabilities, preparation for civic society and democratic government, the development of character and understanding of other cultures."[17] The work of these critics served to strengthen the connection between the humanities and the goal of educating for "engaged citizenship." The emphasis on higher education's role in preparing students for a democratic public life and civic responsibilities is characterized by a rhetorical strategy that I call the "public frame." I define the public frame as *a rhetorical strategy that connects the goals of education with a student's place in a democratic public, civic responsibilities to the care of local and national governance, and the importance of developing critical, ethical, technical, and deliberative capacities for contributing to a shared public life.*[18]

Below I analyze four responses that are representative of broader trends across the corpus. I selected two from individual leaders in higher education and two from major professional organizations and faculty leaders in higher education, all of whom played an active role in publicly responding to the Spellings Report. In particular, I examine the response from the president of St. John's College, Christopher Nelson, who was invited to respond to the Commission at a public roundtable sponsored by the CATO Institute in Washington, DC. I also examine remarks from two prominent academic professional organizations, the Modern Language Association (MLA) and the American Association of University Professors (AAUP).[19] Finally, I also use examples from professor of law and ethics Martha Nussbaum, who made the Spellings Commission a key issue in a series of talks, graduation speeches, and her book *Not for Profit: Why Democracy Needs the Humanities*.

I organize and present the responses according to four common arguments for how higher education serves the public good. The four arguments are each representative of one of the four "public capacities" that colleges and universities can be said to contribute to the public good: (1) critical, (2) ethical, (3) technical, and (4) deliberative. In what follows, I show how these remarks and the public capacities they endorse also point to different ideals of the public sphere.

Critical Capacities for the Public Good

As we saw in chapter 2, president of St. John's College Chris Nelson emerged as an outspoken critic of the Spellings Report's market frame for higher education. At the CATO Institute Forum on the Spellings Commission in Washington, DC, Nelson used his remarks to realign the connection between the individual, education, and the public good. He argues, "Our [liberal arts] colleges serve the public good by helping to bring thoughtful adults into the world—adults who are free to think for themselves, and free to choose paths of action they consider to be best rather than those that are easiest or most popular."[20] Whereas the Spellings Report framed the ends of education for generating the nation's wealth, Nelson repositions the relations between higher education, the state, and the individual. His response also introduces a new value into the debate—duty. And whereas the Spellings Report emphasized "need" and a "crisis," Nelson's emphasis on duty serves to strengthen adherence to the responsibilities institutions of higher education have to free inquiry in a democracy. At the core of this misrepresentation, he argued, was the assumption that freedom in education is about the freedom to choose goods; this understanding of freedom, he argues, is perverse. And he argues that a liberal education—an education that *cultivates* freedom—is valuable because it brings thoughtful, free-thinking people into the world.

Nelson's insistence on serving the public good by bringing "thoughtful adults into the world" is consistent with the ideals of the liberal-free tradition of the liberal arts, wherein people are made free by unburdening themselves from custom and unreflective, inculcated habits and ways of thinking; freedom, in this sense, is to be free from prejudice.[21] To be a good citizen is to exercise this freedom by thinking and acting independently. Nelson distinguishes the relationship between typical acts of citizenship and contributions to the public good. He further argues: "Good citizenship and well-paying jobs, as good as they are, should never be seen by us as more than useful byproducts of our central activity."[22] Nelson's use of the term "byproducts" is significant here because it repositions the values in the debate about the purpose of higher education.[23] The distinction he makes is echoed in Plato's *Republic*, where the ability to govern or attend to the practical affairs of the city justly is believed to be a *byproduct* of an education in the foundational elements of the philosophic life. Nelson, too, emphasizes the importance of learning "foundations and elements."[24] In referencing "foundations and elements," Nelson points to the importance of knowledge that is philosophical, universal, and abiding. He draws from Socrates to argue: "With our students, we accept the wisdom of Socrates, that the unexamined life is not worth living. Another way of putting this is that our students might as well be dead if they are not asking themselves who they are, what kind of world they inhabit, and what their place should be in the scheme of things." Nelson's mention of

Socrates—"the paragon of the liberal tradition"—highlights his privileging of the philosophic, liberal-free tradition.[25] In keeping with previous points, Nelson's remarks serve an invitational function: to show that if we genuinely uphold the value of the individual, of freedom, and of independent thought, then what our democracy needs is grounding in a philosophical education, not the market-driven vocationalism of the Spellings Report.

What is significant about this distinction from a rhetorical perspective is that Nelson does not argue against the ideals of citizenship or even securing well-paying employment but adjusts the *priority* of these values in the hierarchy of values for higher education. This reprioritization is key for changing the terms of the debate. Rather than the Spellings Commission's purpose to "generate wealth" for the nation, Nelson reprioritizes the purpose of higher education as "serving the interest of the individual soul": "We should own up to our commitment to serving the interest of the individual soul. Our duty is to the health of the individual."[26]

By adhering to "the health of the individual soul," Nelson maintains the emphasis on the individual and cultivation of the individual self. This emphasis is important because it creates a foundation for Nelson's critique of the Spellings Commission's recommendation to create a national database that tracks and compares quality of higher education institutions based on earning and completion rates. For Nelson, such a policy solution is unnecessary and misguided because such a database cannot help us understand anything that is of value to the true aims of higher education. In the same way that we must respect the individual autonomy of the individual students, we should respect the individual autonomy of educational institutions that know best how to judge the quality of their education.

Nelson's emphasis on freedom and "free-thinking" is consistent with political liberalism and the critical tradition, which values independent thought. In this way, Nelson uses the public frame to redefine students in the Spellings Report from "consumers" to "free-thinking individuals." These free-thinking individuals have a duty to the public and the state, and they enact good citizenship through their individual actions and choices.

Ethical Capacities for the Public Good

In addition to college presidents such as Nelson who were asked to comment on the report, higher education's professional organizations also used the public frame to draw attention to the Spellings Report's limitations. A notable example came from the Modern Language Association (MLA), the largest humanities professional organization in North America. As highlighted in chapter 2, then-president of the MLA Gerald Graff played an important role in shaping the conversation about the Spellings Report in the field of English and the humanities disciplines more broadly. In an article cowritten with Cathy Birkenstein entitled "Progressive Standardization: How Not to Respond to the Spellings Commission," Graff and Birkenstein argued that most of the responses from colleagues in the academy were unnecessarily reactionary and appealed to individualistic values that were inconsistent with the ideals of democratic education.[27]

Rather than appeal to the primacy of the individual as Nelson did, they argued for a more "progressive" case needed to be made for higher education (see chapter 2). The official Modern Language Association (MLA) public response to the Spellings Report was posted on the organization's website and circulated to its members. It responded to the Spellings Report by noting its lack of attention to the humanities, and therefore lack of attention to ethical capabilities that the humanities help people to cultivate. "The [Spellings] report ignores the humanities' role in training workers for the new global knowledge economy and their ability to help citizens think more imaginatively, feel greater sympathy with others, and make sounder moral judgments. Our society needs scientists, engineers, and doctors who are not only technically proficient but also conscious of the moral, social, and human consequences of their decisions."[28]

Here the MLA uses the public frame to emphasize how the Commission's vision for higher education failed to address the moral and ethical dimensions that the humanities provide. The MLA response does not change the fundamental terms and aim of the Spellings Report in reframing the purpose of higher education; instead, the MLA accepts the fundamental premise that higher education "trains workers for the new global knowledge economy," but instead emphasizes how we need workers to become more ethical and conscious of their actions.[29]

The effect of statements like the MLA's was to solidify the connection between higher education, the humanities, and the cultivation of moral subjects with appropriately cultivated feelings and emotions. It emphasizes the need for the development of empathy and for social and cultural awareness. Most importantly, it emphasizes the way that the building of a shared society—not just an economy—requires a broader range of human capacities, which higher education helps to cultivate.

Technical Capacities for the Public Good

A third use of the public frame focused on higher education's role in training experts with the technical knowledge that contributes to public issues. This emphasis on technical capacities is advocated for in the response circulated by the American Association of University Professors (AAUP).[30] The AAUP was especially active in mobilizing its membership and circulating many responses to the Commission Report to the Commission and the AAUP membership. The following example is drawn from the response circulated internally to their membership, strengthening adherence to the organization's shared values: "The AAUP affirms the central importance of higher education in enabling an informed citizenry to participate in civic and political life and the key role played by academic researchers in creating knowledge that has direct consequences for economic innovation and successful public policy."[31] By emphasizing an "informed citizenry" and the role that researchers play in "creating knowledge," the AAUP appeals to a model of citizenship that relies on technical expertise for making policy decisions, and it promotes access to the public sphere by sharing expert knowledge to a wider, nonexpert public. The AAUP argues that it "has long advocated public policies that make higher education fully accessible to all those who are qualified to benefit from it, that aim to improve the quality of higher education based on academic values, and that adequately fund research to stimulate the growth and dissemination of knowledge."[32] Like other uses of the public frame, AAUP's response draws attention to the multiple purposes and strengths of what universities offer the public good beyond job training or global competitiveness. The organization's response emphasizes improving the quality of higher education "based on academic values" and serves as a reminder that values from the business or corporate world should not dictate research or teaching priorities. Unlike the MLA response, the AAUP's response highlights "dissemination of knowledge" rather than moral feeling or commitment, which allows for a kind of neutral position on ethical issues. In this way, it reflects the values and ideals of a technocratic model of the public sphere, which prioritizes technical knowledge in decision-making.

Deliberative Capacities for the Public Good

A fourth use of the public frame highlights the need for citizens to be attentive to the needs of others and to be able to engage with others critically and charitably around issues that may not appear to be matters of shared concern. While sharing some aspects of the ethical or critical capacities, this use of the public frame to highlight deliberative capacities brings two values into focus: listening and imaginative capacity.

In the Spellings case, this use of the public frame was represented in statements from Martha Nussbaum, professor of law and philosophy at the University of Chicago. In invited lectures, graduation speeches, and other writings, Nussbaum emerged as one of the most publicly visible scholarly voices who spoke out against the Spellings Commission and defended the value of the humanities in higher education. Nussbaum's speeches were pivotal in generating concern—mostly from faculty—about the "crisis" of the humanities in higher education. Her public statements culminated in the 2011 book *Not for Profit: Why Democracy Needs the Humanities*, a manifesto that argues for the humanistic, as opposed to economic, benefits of an education steeped in the humanities.[33]

Like other critics at that time, Nussbaum denounced the aims of the Spellings Commission's overemphasis on vocational education, with little attention to the role of the liberal arts and humanities. But unlike Nelson's emphasis on critical capacities to act as individuals, or the MLA's emphasis on the capacity to be aware of ethical concerns, or the AAUP's emphasis on technical knowledge, Nussbaum introduced a somewhat different perspective on public life: the need for citizens to learn to make public arguments and to deliberate and make decisions together, which for Nussbaum requires the ability to argue with and listen to those who are very different in the public sphere. She maintains that "democracy needs citizens who can reason together about their choices rather than just trade claims and counter-claims."[34] Nussbaum's argument rests on an important distinction between *making* public arguments and *listening* to them: it is not enough to have a public sphere for deliberation if there is no expectation of listening and being heard.

Our ability to listen and deliberate also requires that we have a different kind of knowledge and that we seek to understand those who are different from us. According to Nussbaum, this commitment to cultivating difference impacts what should be taught in the classroom: "As citizens within each nation we are frequently called upon to make decisions that require some understanding of racial and ethnic and religious groups in that nation, and of the situation of its women and its sexual minorities. We also need to understand how issues such as agriculture, human rights, climate change, business and industry, and, of course, violence and terrorism, are generating discussions that bring people together from various nations."[35] Rather than learning universal philosophical principles, or the technical knowledge of disciplinary expertise, Nussbaum emphasizes how higher education helps students to cultivate *imagination*. The value of imagination is highlighted in Nussbaum's speeches, where she emphasizes the importance of seeing the world from the perspective of others. As Nussbaum argues: "Citizens cannot think well on the basis of factual knowledge alone.... Good citizenship requires that we challenge our imaginative capacity, learning what the world looks like from the point of view of groups we typically try not to see."[36] Learning to see the world from another's perspective is a form of empathy, not unlike the kind of empathy that the MLA statement emphasized. Nussbaum reframes the Spellings Commission's emphasis on "skills" to "work faster" with a different social understanding of how to relate to other human beings. But what also seems different in Nussbaum's formulation is how she emphasizes "the point of view of groups we typically try not to see." Most notably, our goal for higher education should not be cultivating a sense of competition with known others, but a deeper understanding of how others have been marginalized and oppressed. This requires the development of a kind of social knowledge that deliberation makes possible.[37] In this way, she connects the aims of higher education with an imperative that higher education seek cooperation and social justice, rather than competition in a market imperative.

Problems with the Public Frame: Unity and Plurality

In the Spellings case, higher education advocates were largely effective in mobilizing support for their position by using the public frame to demonstrate the limitations of the Spellings Commission's market framing for higher education. Across these representative examples of the public frame, advocates in higher education highlighted the plurality of ways that it serves the public good by helping students cultivate critical, ethical, technical, and deliberative capacities. What I call the public frame strategy offers an important advantage in policy debates: it can be used to create or strengthen a unified message and framework of argument for the many ways that higher education serves the public good.

But the use of a public frame raises problems for higher education advocates, too, insofar as its unity can elide important differences in how individual arguers envision the public good and the kind of democratic public higher education ought to help make possible. So, when advocates say that higher education is a public good, we should also ask, what kind of public are they assuming to prepare students to participate in? Here I take inspiration

BUILDING A PUBLIC FRAME 71

Table 4 Five models of the public sphere commonly invoked in debates about US higher education.

	Purpose of public discourse	Required knowledge	Style of discourse
Interest-based model	To persuade in order maximize self-interest	Market principles; business savvy	Bargaining; market and industry driven
Liberal model	To achieve consensus	Universal philosophical principles	Critical-rational, argument
Communitarian model	To create a sense of community cohesion	Common values, morals, history among a plurality	Local, vernacular language norms
Technocratic model	To disseminate technical information	Disciplinary, scientific facts	Expert discourse
Deliberative model	To co-create social knowledge, understanding	Normative ethical principles; knowledge of diverse cultures	Broad notion of argument; narrative; empathy and listening

from Patricia Roberts-Miller's *Deliberate Conflict*, where she observes that many of our pedagogical disagreements can be accounted for by understanding teachers' competing visions for how to prepare students to participate in public life.[38] In table 4, I adapt Roberts-Miller's work to highlight fundamental differences between five corresponding visions of public life we often invoke when claiming and that higher education is a public good: the interest-based, liberal, communitarian, technocratic, and deliberative.[39] In my reading of her work, these competing visions of the public sphere each have three defining characteristics, including *purpose of public discourse* (what is the assumed purpose of discourse and argument in the public sphere?), required *knowledge* (what types of knowledge are required for citizens to participate in the public sphere?), and *style of discourse* (what types of argument or communicative engagement are permitted in the public sphere?).

While Roberts-Miller's book clarifies the public stakes of pedagogical debates about writing curriculum, I find that her insight about the differences between our ideals of the public sphere also helps to bring clarity to policy debates about higher education and the public good more broadly. Table 4 highlights a range of competing assumptions and ideals that advocates implicitly bring to the table when discussing the *purpose* or main goal of higher education. It also highlights the way that the four public capacities highlighted in the Spellings case—the critical, ethical, technical, and deliberative capacities—draw their persuasive power from different ideals of the public sphere.

One limitation of table 4 to note is that, in trying to draw clear boundaries between these visions, the categories obscure how people usually hold multiple goals for higher education and different ideal types of public capacities that it could help students cultivate at different times. But the point in offering a taxonomy is to draw our attention to how the supposed unity of "the public frame" is challenged by a plurality of different ideals for how higher education prepares students to engage in public life. Table 4 also helps us identify the kind(s) of public sphere and citizen we or others invoke when making the case for higher education as a public good.

Additionally, to use the public frame in policy debates, it is important we understand these possible points of difference that may lead to disagreement. In what follows, I describe four challenges that can arise when using the public frame in policy debates about the value of higher education.

Individuals and the Collective

The first challenge the public frame raises regards the relationship between the individual and society, with its implications for how we understand the relationship between private and public interests. We can see this tension demonstrated in both Nelson's remarks and the MLA's response to the Spellings Commission. In strengthening a commitment to the value of the individual and the importance of "free inquiry," Nelson's argument aligns itself with a longer rhetorical pattern of higher education advocacy emphasizing "free inquiry" and "institutional autonomy," values that define the relationship between individual students, individual institutions of higher education, and the federal government.[40]

In higher education policy today, we also see the tension between the individual and collective emerge in debates about funding allocation models. Consider, for example, how much funding for US higher education is already allocated directly to individual students, who then decide which institutions to attend and pay (via Pell Grants, federally backed student loans, etc.). In contrast to K–12 education funding, federal policies that govern higher education in the United States have traditionally focused on research funding or aid for the *individual*. These and other material constraints are why it seems reasonable that students and their parents or guardians will approach higher education *as* a private good. As state funding for institutions shrinks and individuals take on more personal debt, students also naturally view education as more a private good or investment for themselves than for society. But, as Newfield argues, even as state governments cut funding and create new policies that erode our sense of higher education as a public good, our colleges still make significant contributions to the collective public good, which austerity policies obscure.

Ethical Responsibility Without Moralizing

The second challenge the public frame raises regards the question of ethics, and whose ethics should guide public policy decision-making. A common critique of the liberal model's emphasis on individuality and neutrality is that it obfuscates the individual's moral and ethical responsibility. Likewise, a common critique of the communitarian model is that it can result in enclaving, meaning one potential danger of the communitarian ideal of the public sphere is that it counterintuitively risks universalizing the ethical particularities of one community over other communities.[41] In the context of higher education policy, we see the issue of universalizing ethical particularities emerge when different sectors of higher education—which consists of research universities, public state colleges, liberal arts colleges, community colleges, and more—speak as though their sector of higher education represents the whole of higher education.

We also see issues related to ethical responsibility with the rise of for-profit colleges and universities. For example, proponents of for-profit colleges often argue they fill a gap in the education marketplace by primarily serving students that the nonprofit institutions do not. In this way, proponents of for-profit schools argue that they serve an ethical function in a market-based society. In contrast, critics argue that for-profit colleges are predatory and seek to exploit and profit off both individual students and the federal government.[42] In such debates, there has been a tendency to moralize the issues or to shame those who seek for-profit degrees or who offer them. But the challenge here is to introduce an ethics of public responsibility for our institutions, such that individuals can make different choices about their education.

Expertise Without Elitism

The third challenge raised by the public frame concerns citizen expertise. While the public frame can be used to honor the technical capacities that faculty and student researchers bring to policy debates, it can also be misconstrued as higher education retreating to the ivory tower or perpetuating the perception that its experts know better than everyone else. This view of democratic participation relies on a weak version of a technocratic model of the public sphere. It is a model of the public sphere that, in its most extreme form, assumes that experts should make policy decisions for everyone else who is not as well-informed.

The problem with idealizing technical capacities is that it can, in some cases, result in an elitist type of enclaving. In the context of higher education policy, one sees the possibility for this type of elitism in a distorted version of the AAUP's response. Though it may seem unfair to characterize the AAUP's response as endorsing a form of technocracy (I do not think it does in this case), it certainly could be when it is argued that the public sphere functions primarily for the *dissemination* of expert information, and the assumption that people make decisions after listening to information from experts. However, the forms of knowledge and expertise of faculty include not only technical knowledge of policy issues but also situated knowledge about teaching and the best ways to facilitate student learning. The challenge is to use the public frame to emphasize the relevant expertise that teachers and researchers in higher education bring to policy issues, while recognizing the other forms of expertise that other stakeholders could bring.

Deliberation with Difference

Finally, the fourth challenge raised by the public frame regards the range of interpretive variability for "deliberation" or argument. The goal of the deliberative model is to encourage citizens to uphold values such as listening, cultivating difference, and furthering imaginative capability to problem solve. The deliberative public sphere assumes that "public deliberation leads to better and more just political decisions only if there is equal access on the part of people with genuinely different points of view, the opportunity to make arguments (rather than simply assertions), the time for exploration of different options, and a cultural milieu that values listening."[43]

So, just as the liberal model of the public sphere was theorized to implement argument and dialogue in response to an interest-based model, the deliberative model of the public sphere is another attempt to do just this, but with a presumably broader notion of "argument." The deliberative public sphere puts public deliberation at its core. But unlike the liberal model, it values difference, and embraces it rather than tries to transcend it. Iris Marion

Young summarizes it this way: "Deliberative democracy differs from other attitudes and practices in democratic politics in that it exhorts participants to be concerned not only with their own interests but to listen to and take account of the interests of others insofar as these are compatible with justice."[44]

One criticism is that models of deliberative democracy have little guidance for seriously asking the question if its deliberations are occurring in a closed or distorted way; in fact, it has to presume they are not in order to deliberate in the first place. Put another way, the deliberative model lacks a theory, or a way to step outside ideology, to "give an account of the genealogy of discourses and their manner of helping to constitute the way individuals see themselves and their social world. For most deliberative democrats, discourse seems to be ... innocent."[45] Thus we need equal footing among members for there to be a truly deliberative public sphere. But this is rarely the case in institutions of higher education, which differ dramatically as regards the constituents they serve. It is for this reason that we must try to consider and listen for the perspectives of those we do not typically hear.

In the context of higher education policy, achieving deliberative conditions is difficult, since there are varying degrees of power and resources that allow people of different institutions to participate in the first place. The challenge is always to find ways to work across difference, or else we run the risk of making policies that benefit only the few, or policies that fail to capture the diversity of people and perspectives that could strengthen US higher education. The more that individual institutions of higher education stay in their own enclaves (Ivies, state colleges, small liberal arts colleges, etc.), the less they are able to deliberate about issues that concern the whole of higher education with its plurality of mission types.

Modeling Public Work

One consequence of the Spellings Commission's emphasis on numerical metrics of accountability is that it invited a defensive response from higher education, one fundamentally grounded in government skepticism. Another consequence was that it revealed a weakening sense of trust between higher education and policymakers. As Muller observes, "The quest for numerical metrics of accountability is particularly attractive in cultures marked by low social trust."[46]

In the previous examples, leaders in higher education used the public frame to shift from an emphasis on higher education as a means of acquiring skills to compete in a global market to higher education as means to cultivating capacities for contributing productively to a public life. Such advocates did not just argue for higher education as a public good, they *modeled* their understanding of what contributing to the public good should look like. In this way, they exemplify a point made in *The New Rhetoric* that when using epideictic rhetoric—the rhetoric of praise and blame—the rhetor becomes an educator.[47] Epideictic moments became educational moments when those in higher education were called to remind others *about the proper role of higher education in a democracy*.

The Spellings controversy also highlighted the way that ignoring the value of the humanities was to dismiss a range of values that higher education as a whole offers a democratic public. The case also demonstrated how imperative it is that leaders in higher education continually debate and strengthen adherence to the nonmarket values of higher education and how higher education can play a role in strengthening democratic values. What is notable in the Spellings case is how the institutional autonomy argument and the technical expertise argument tapped into well-worn arguments that have been used to keep higher education from being subjected to new regulatory reforms. The effect of other arguments for the ethical and deliberative capacities had some effect, too, but appeared in very different ways, such as influencing later reports like *A Crucible Moment: College Learning and Democracy's Future*.[48]

The Spellings case was significant for another reason: it united faculty and those in higher education in a common goal, despite the great variety of educational institutions that make up US higher education and very different models of education at each type of institution. At a public roundtable on the humanities in the years following the Spellings Commission, for example, Judith Butler remarked on the confusion of the new age of education policy: "Indeed, part of what has become confusing is that those who dismiss the value of the humanities often present themselves as innovators, ushering in a new age, fighting against recalcitrant and hermetic forces within the university. It is a moment, oddly, when the old-style conservatives find themselves joining with their erstwhile foes on the critical left."[49] In the Spellings case, even the faculty and professional organizations that may have been on opposite sides of the culture wars of the 1980s and 1990s worked in tandem to advocate for the public good of higher education. And it was this rhetorical public frame that allowed advocates to unite around a commitment to the public good without necessarily having to elide important differences their educational approaches or the diversity of education types that comprise US higher education.

An important lesson of the Spellings case was that higher education leaders today cannot just be skilled managers of institutions and fundraising—they must be *skilled rhetoricians* who can engage multiple publics in serious reflection about what constitutes our public good. Put another way, they must be educators who can help cultivate a broad sense of public responsibility and obligation and can help others to deliberate about public matters. The challenge is, How do we train and prepare educators to lead in this way? How do we educate them to be committed to a democratic public, rather than to splinter off and try to create their own enclave with their own utopia? In the next chapter, I turn to how the question of higher education's public purposes can be an important guide for training new leadership in higher education. I offer the *higher education leader as a public advocate* who is committed to a deliberative model of policy development, both within the university and outside of it with policymakers and public stakeholders.

4

LEADING FOR THE PUBLIC GOOD

Public life is always a pedagogical project—and an imaginative and aspirational one at that.
—Jennifer Clifton

The Spellings Commission controversy, the recommendations of its report, and its policy legacy has been followed by a leadership crisis in higher education: who can—or would even want to—lead in higher education advocacy efforts under such conditions, and under increasing public scrutiny? When Senator Lamar Alexander, US senator and a former college president himself, testified before the Spellings Commission in 2005, he positioned himself as someone with an experienced perspective on the challenges of higher education leadership. He explained how people would often ask, "What's harder: being governor of a state, a member of a president's cabinet, or president of a university?" To which he responded, "Obviously, you've never been president of a university, or you wouldn't ask such a question."[1]

The leadership constraints and challenges facing higher education are unique and complex. In higher education today, there are three things that a public leader must know how to speak about: (1) the ends of education (why we do what we do); (2) how higher education must function in order to meet those ends; and (3) to whom higher education is accountable and why. To become more effective advocates for the public value of higher education, leaders will need a different kind of guidance than the manuals or organizational charts of stakeholders, budget primers, and tips for structuring meeting agendas. Advocates will also need something somewhat different than critiques of the university or historicist descriptions of higher education's protracted public gutting. While these types of books are all important and even necessary for conceptualizing the problems that higher education faces, they rarely offer help understanding what it means to start doing public advocacy and affect policymaking.

The Spellings controversy illuminates that effectively advocating for higher education as a public good requires more than a messaging campaign run by a university's marketing or PR department. It requires a reorientation and responsiveness from teaching and research faculty, board leadership, and college and university administrators to the work of being public educators about higher education. It also requires advocates to have rhetorical capabilities, including but not limited to the those exhibited in the previous chapters of this book. For example, it requires that we understand the implications of style in policymaking and seek together to counter the managerial style as the only way of making policy (chapter 1). It requires that we attend to techniques of argumentation in policymaking that can help prioritize accountability to a range of public values and outcomes instead of just market values (chapter 2). And it requires that we have shared starting places for arguments that can help to frame higher education as a fundamentally public, rather than private, good (chapter 3). This chapter offers an alternative model for the higher education leader equipped with such capabilities that we need today: the higher education leader as *public advocate*.

The higher education leader as public advocate approaches their advocacy work not merely in response to an expert's framing of the public's concerns, but as an *active co-creator of shared public life*. In other words, the higher education leader as public advocate recognizes the constitutive role that universities already play in creating our shared sense of public life and offers an approach for remaking it with the public's aims as its priority.

This type of advocate in higher education contexts should work to more directly influence education policy than current models permit, but I want to be clear that we need not all become policy experts, cultural historians of higher education, or run for public office (though it would be helpful to have elected representatives with backgrounds in higher education). This distinction is important. Policy experts are experts about policy, whereas most of us involved in higher education are not experts in public policy. Policy experts tend to be professionals "whose authority is built on a claim to mediate an encounter among various forms of power."[2] Instead, the higher education leader as public advocate that this book seeks to cultivate should be an expert *in how to interpret shared problems, how to draw out and name the values and* stakes in a policy situation, and how to facilitate deliberation about higher education policies.

In what follows, I discuss two recent trends in the literature on leadership and the future of higher education where each tends to orient leaders toward their "public" role: the revolutionary model and the reformist model of higher education. I compare and critique the visions to help clarify what makes the public advocate model distinct. I then outline three characteristics of what a higher education leader as a public advocate does. Finally, I emphasize why public deliberation is key to future advocacy for higher education and suggest one model for how to support deliberative decision-making in higher education.

Revolutionary and Reformist Models for Higher Education

Since the Spellings Commission, there have been two general trends in the literature on higher education leadership and higher education reform: the revolutionary and the reformist models. The first, often led by self-proclaimed futurists who work in higher education, has focused on how to either "disrupt," "unbundle," or "abolish" the system of higher education, since it is already on the brink of becoming, or perceived to be, dystopian.[3] The shared metaphor driving its model of change is one of revolution, as grounded in a utopian impulse. And its arguments tend to be based on theories and ideas about reviving an imaginary past as higher education's future or about predicting the future and how higher education—"the most fractured institution of all"—can emerge like the phoenix.

Former St. John's College president Pano Kanelos's 2021 substack, entitled "We Can't Wait for Universities to Fix Themselves. So We're Starting a New One," is emblematic of the "unbundling" approach.[4] Kanelos's screed against higher education explains the exigency for creating a totally new type of college, University of Austin, a college for the future that is at the same time, "retro—perhaps even countercultural—in an era of massive open online courses and distance learning to build an actual school in an actual building with as *few* screens as possible."[5] While there are many dubious aspects of Kanelos's defense, especially in what he chooses to pass over, what stands out most is his title, where it is clear that he and those who signed up with him draw on the familiar trope of blame in higher education. What such futurist models also tend to have in common is that they blame the illiberalism of students and the public, but especially universities as entities that should "fix themselves."

The announcement of University of Austin is representative of a growing and pervasive antipublic attitude in higher education reform. Rather than work with or try to support the public mission of existing colleges or universities for the public good, these groups want to start new ones for their own good. Of course, few educators have not at some point dreamed of starting their own university. But the attempt to create a utopia can be dangerous in a democracy if an idealized past or future becomes a way to avoid a shared public responsibility for higher education.[6] Despite University of Austin's claims that it is dedicated to democracy, their announcement seems more emblematic of enclaving than of public-building.

Following a similar utopian impulse are other higher education futurists who argue that, rather than look to the past for the future we would want to have, we need to instead "disrupt" the old models of higher education and more collectively envision emergent new ones, usually in line with changing economies. A standout example of this type of proposal is higher education consultant David Staley's 2019 book *Alternative Universities: Speculative Design for Innovation in Higher Education*. In fact, Staley uses the Spellings Commission on Higher Education to justify such changes, recognizing the way that the Spellings controversy has invited a trend of idealists to critique higher education and thus call for its "disruptive innovation." Staley correctly acknowledges that some of the claims in the Spellings Report, those that characterized higher education as "slow to change and reluctant to innovate," are not really consistent with the history of US higher education. Higher education in the United States has frequently changed and adapted to changing circumstances. So, Staley concludes, "The problem is not that universities are lacking in innovation, but rather that they suffer from a *poverty of imagination*."[7]

Staley's book focuses on speculative, imagined versions of what universities *could be*, such as the Platform University, the Microcollege, the Humanities Think Tank, the Nomad University, and others. What I think Staley gets right is his emphasis on imagination, especially his belief that we can and should envision models of higher education beyond the corporate, entrepreneurial, and bureaucratic university. But Staley's book raises an interesting challenge: where do such imaginings come from? In emphasizing the need to imagine more, we are also left wondering not only where these ideas of the future come from, but also how to use them. How are alternative models of the university useful beyond the musings of some education futurists?

What seems missing from thought experiments such as Staley's is a clear sense of democratic values and public commitment. Despite being trained in universities, revolutionaries imagine futures where universities are not the universities we have today. But what might be the impact on people and our sense of public life *without* the university? And how can we facilitate deliberation about these imagined alternatives in a way that prioritizes values of equity and commitment to a public good? For most people in leadership positions in higher education today—department heads, deans, provosts, and presidents—it probably feels as though there is little time to devote to such thought experiments of imagination. I am therefore interested in a somewhat different question: how do we create the conditions for people to imagine and to deliberate about the values of alternative universities, while continuing to be accountable to its public aims?

In contradistinction to the futurists, the second major trend in higher education literature tends to emphasize reforms of current institutions, rather than a complete revolution or fundamental change in kind, while keeping an emphasis on higher education's public mission. At the core of this approach are those who argue that, in dealing with public scrutiny, we have sometimes succumbed to an antipublic narrative, rather than fully appreciating the public value that our colleges and universities already do offer and their potential to offer more. For example, instead of trying to disrupt, abolish, or unbundle institutions of higher education, Jason Owen-Smith argues in *Research Universities and the Public Good* that the strengths of US public research institutions—however messy and complicated—still far outweigh its problems.[8] Owen-Smith makes the case for the public value of research universities in particular via the use of three metaphors: universities as *networks*, universities as community *anchors*, and universities as *hubs* linking communities.

For those in the reformist camp, we do not need totally new visions of higher education so much as we need to help members of the public understand what higher education already does well and what it could do better. That is, reformists tend to argue that those who call for revolutionary changes in higher education are generally mistaken, or that they are not aware of how higher education *actually* works. Understanding the operations of higher education is immensely complicated and requires not only competencies in expert to nonexpert communication, but also deep-situated experience.

A second type of reformist focuses on the need for better education about how colleges and universities operate. In *How to Run a College*, Brian Mitchell and Joseph King argue that the key to higher education's survival in the future is the *education of its stakeholders*. "The education of the stakeholders in higher education will mean that these groups understand the comprehensive interconnection between the people, programs, and facilities that shape an institution's direction. Survival means understanding how the pieces work together.... It begins with education."[9] They go on to argue that the hardest part of governance is helping diverse groups of stakeholders understand these interconnections. In particular, they stress the difficulty of working with boards of trustees, who are in one sense representative of the members of the public. Mitchell and King offer a critical assessment of most boards, who tend to be "uninformed, oversubscribed, and heavily dependent on alumni members who often view a college as a personal fiefdom. They meet infrequently, draw too narrowly from a list of candidates drawn from a self-perpetuating pool of former classmates and donors, and fail to prepare their officers and committee chairs for the business of governance."[10] This sobering portrayal of university boards, if they are indicative of the public, provides a sense of the vulnerabilities and challenges that higher education leaders face in cultivating spaces of trust both within the university itself and outside it.

Finally, a third type of higher education reformist focuses less on the organizational structure of the institution and more on the forms of education that it offers. Such reform work can be seen in books such as Cathy Davidson's *The New Education*. Davidson finds inspiration in former Harvard president Charles Eliot's *Atlantic* essay "The New Education," which was written to usher in higher education for the industrial age, a form of education that we still have today with majors, grades, departments, and professional schools. Admittedly, Davidson's work, with her emphasis on a "new" and "revolutionary" education, may sound more appropriately situated in the futurist camp; indeed, she does argue that "to revolutionize the university, we don't just need a model. We need a movement."[11] However, Davidson fundamentally affirms the public mission of higher education and seeks to strengthen the infrastructure we have today rather than to rebuild on its ashes. Davidson argues that it is those within higher education who need to work to design what's new and revolutionary about it, rather than cede it to futurist venture capitalists or other disruptors, despite how well-meaning.

Ultimately, the key difference between the revolutionaries and the reformers of higher education rests on whether they see the public advantages of universities as they are currently configured outweighing its problems. Whereas futurists tend to think that higher education is so broken or inadequate that we must transcend it, go beyond it, or return to ancient models of education completely, reformists try to strengthen the higher education we have, arguing for its underrealized potential. While neither approach is totally wrong in its assessment of higher education's problems, my concern is that most futurist arguments seek to pass over rather than to acknowledge what is already strong and promising about the university as its currently configured and the good it has done for some, despite the fact that it should do better for all. A corollary issue is that many attempts at revolutionary alternatives for education seem basically like versions of the disciplines or many programs that already exist in universities today in miniature.

The leadership model I am putting forward for higher education advocacy shares some of the concerns of the revolutionaries but may seem to rest more squarely in the reformist camp. We need collective reimagining for higher education. Imagination is essential to leadership work. And we will need to create the conditions for such collective reimagining. It is crucial to keep imagining that things could get better, and furthermore, to imagine how they might get better.[12] Higher education leaders cannot merely be public spokespeople for our current model of higher education, insofar as it is a model that emphasizes private return on investment more than public outcomes and its return on investment for society. To that end, I argue that the higher education leader as public advocate is someone who *convenes local publics, interprets shared problems, and facilitates deliberation about higher education policies* in a way that builds trust among stakeholders and public constituents.

The Higher Ed Leader as Local Public Convener

Foremost, the higher education leader as public advocate is a *convener of local publics*. Unlike other leadership models based on different ideals of the public sphere (see table 4), which focus on visionary leadership and technical expertise, including the circulation of technical knowledge for a lay public (technical model) or casting critical judgment on a public issue (critical model), the higher education leader as a public advocate understands that public discourse is what Michael Warner describes as a kind of "poetic worldmaking," which requires deliberative engagements with the others (deliberative model). By poetic world-making I mean the public advocate does not only offer an ethical perspective on an issue of public concern, but instead makes an issue ethical by *making* it a matter of public concern (ethical model).

Key to being a convener of public concerns includes cultivating rhetorical strategies for offering a public frame (chapter 3) for interpreting and understanding what institutions of higher education ultimately do, how they work, and how they might better serve the public rather than the student or themselves. While there is obviously much disagreement about how to define higher education as a public good—or even how to define a public good generally—even invoking a public good *topos* can be a powerful and productive way of habituating people to think and argue beyond private concerns.[13] Prompting people to explain or justify *how* a policy solution might serve the public good can be useful in helping others to think of themselves as participating in a shared public life about higher education.

Distinguish Technical from Adaptive Problems

Higher education leaders as public advocates should approach policy issues—including the issue of higher education support and funding—as *adaptive challenges* (Heifetz), not technical problems. Or put another way, such leaders should recognize and define the difference between technical problems and adaptive challenges.[14] This means cultivating an ability to discern cases where the appearance of a technical problem is really an adaptive challenge, or one that deals primarily with values, behaviors, beliefs, and relationships rather than inputs and outputs. For example, in the Spellings case, when policy problems were framed as "lack of information," the policy solution was to create a database of information. However, as advocates in higher education tried to make clear, the problem-framing for issues of access, affordability, and the quality of higher education was so poorly defined that it could not be resolved with a technical solution like a database. Being human, we may always have a lack of knowledge about some issues—but knowledge is not the same as information, and certainly not the types of information that the Spellings Commission proposed to solve higher education's various problems.

Facilitate Trust Through Deliberation

Finally, the higher education leader as public advocate facilitates deliberation as a builder and practitioner of trust. As Robert Asen argues in *Democracy, Deliberation, and Education*, trust is not "a precondition or an outcome of deliberation" but "a relational practice" that "unfolds through deliberation."[15] What is at stake is partially about actual decision-making, but it's also about others *feeling* included and *valued* as part of a decision in the world they are helping make, which builds trust. As Asen observes, "When people perceive that deliberation does not matter—either because their interlocutors have initiated deliberation simply to provide political cover for a decision that already has been made or because interlocutors will conduct their future actions without any reference to relevant deliberations—they may substitute feelings of cynicism and alienation for the practices of trust."[16] Unfortunately, for many leaders in higher education today, especially those who try to manage others rather than support or empower them, the performance of deliberative engagement is more frustrating than rewarding. And they have perhaps had very good reason to feel this way based on prior experience. Indeed, in the Spellings case, many in higher education perceived the public deliberations as a political cover-up or subterfuge for a set of technical policy decisions that had already been made by management, rather than a genuine opportunity to consider alternative policy solutions. Such a perception significantly strained possibilities for the practices of trust-building.[17] Despite this, I would like to argue that deliberation in the Spellings case was still important because it forced people to be public about their commitments. It also drew out a wider range of perspectives that are essential for beneficent and effective policymaking.

In contrast to the managerial style of the Spellings Report (see chapter 1), which prioritized the values of business and the marketplace, technical approaches to problem-solving, and an emphasis on speed and efficiency of decision-making, the style I am modeling offers something much different. In lieu of metaphors of business and the marketplace, which delimit the human imagination to capitalist realism, the public advocate for higher education argues for the public good of higher education as places of public learning that are concerned first and foremost with knowledge making for the good of the public. In lieu of strictly technical approaches to problem-solving, such a leader tries to distinguish adaptive challenges that higher education faces, then goes out of their way to facilitate deliberation about policy changes to address it, one that brings multiple stakeholders into collective problem-solving. And the public advocate emphasizes awareness of timing and the importance of time and deliberation as an infrastructure need, rather than emphasizing speed and efficiency in all things as simply a "matter of fact."[18] To achieve this, the higher education leader as public advocate must become someone who facilitates practices of trust-building with higher education and the public, rather than a manager, futurist, or revolutionary with a "vision" for others to follow.

To be clear, as large organizations, institutions of higher education do require skilled managers to help address decisions about budgeting, space planning, and organization. But we encounter problems when it is assumed that managerial approaches to problem-solving can substitute for, or be adequate for, addressing adaptive challenges and for public policy situations that by nature require deliberation. The deliberative model of leadership recognizes that such an awareness requires, first, rhetorical training and careful judgment, and second, the ability to disassociate between problems whose solutions could be deliberated about and problems that are genuinely technical and require other types of knowledge (see chapter 3).

Building Relationships Through Deliberative Spaces

I emphasize cultivating rhetorical skills because rhetoric has always been part of traditions focused not only on what is, but what *could be*. Helping people within and outside higher education to deliberate about an unknown future, and facing up to our limitations in knowing it, requires skill and expertise beyond managerial aphorisms and thought experiments. "Properly understood," Danielle Allen argues, "rhetoric is not [merely] a list of stylistic rules but an outline of the radical commitment to other citizens that is needed for a just democratic politics."[19] That radical commitment to other citizens depends on a willingness to strengthen our deliberative, public capacities.

This model of leadership focuses on the *public, deliberative* aspects needed for higher education leadership because so many other approaches to leadership emphasize charisma or other interpersonal skills as idealized leadership traits. Take, for example, how Stephen M. Gavazzi and E. Gordon Gee in *Land-Grant Universities for the Future: Higher Education for the Public Good* use the metaphor of marriage to characterize the relationship between higher education and the public at large. In drawing the comparison between a good higher education leader and a good marriage partner, they ask, "After all, if you are not routinely asking your partner what they want you to do, how can you know for sure that you are providing what your partner needs in actuality? If you are offering only what you assume your partner needs, some serious errors in judgment can (and often) do occur."[20] Gavazzi and Gee use these questions to suggest that universities need to be working with local communities to ensure mutual needs are being met. For experienced college presidents, this marriage metaphor perhaps resonates, given that both had much experience cultivating relationships with community members, alumni, parents, and other stakeholders for higher education. In some ways, this metaphor makes a lot of sense for understanding how to cultivate relationships and responsiveness. But one obvious limitation is that it suggests a romantic sentiment or sense of obligation that is likely missing in most relationships between universities and their publics.

In contrast to the marriage metaphor, a more helpful metaphor for describing the relationship between higher education and its publics is one of *political friendship*. Allen defines political friendship as "not mainly (or not only) a sentiment of fellow-feeling for other citizens," but "a way of acting in respect to [each other]: friendship, known to all, defines the normative aspirations. One doesn't even have to like one's fellow citizens in order to act toward them as a political friend."[21] Allen's emphasis on political friendship as a habit of practice and showing respect for one another provides a more helpful metaphor for policy development because emphasizes reciprocity, attentiveness, care, and the human effort of relationship-building, without a romantic sentiment. By using the model of political friendship as a norm, leaders in higher education can cultivate and learn to practice habits of deliberation and listening, which are so crucial for building trust. Let us look together at the three most important reasons why this deliberative approach is necessary for the higher education leader as public advocate.

Invention of New Ideas

First, deliberation allows groups to discover and invent new ideas. It can help in facilitating collective imagining, and thus lead to a more shared imagination for the future of higher education. As Aristotle observed, a whole is always greater than the sum of its parts.[22] Necessarily, there are ideas and commitments that can emerge in collective imagining that simply cannot emerge when imagining on our own, no matter how innovative each of us might think we are alone. Current theorists and critics of higher education emphasize that imagination is the most important component for envisioning a new future. Despite their limits, calls for imagination are typically short-sighted in the number of parts they include. On this view, the problem with imagination is a problem of ethics. Imagination without consideration of others is problematic, but imagination *without* others will not help us figure out workable solutions to shared problems that involve others. In fact, imagination and deliberation about it are perhaps more interconnected than we may think, and collective imagination comes about through the inventive practice of deliberation together. Collective imagination requires a kind of deliberation with others across differences.

Bolstering Shared Commitments

Second, a deliberative approach to higher education is necessary because imagining solutions to its problems together can bolster commitment to actualize them through effective policymaking and public advocacy efforts. As Asen explains: "Deliberation cannot eliminate contingency—for this may be an inescapable element of a shared social world—but, to the extent that participants heed deliberation, it may bolster their commitment to a decision, thus enabling people to anticipate the consequences of their actions."[23] The stakes of sharing a commitment to a shared vision among higher education's stakeholders is apparent in the Spellings case, whose accountability measures were fiercely objected to by many who, in principle, were not opposed to accountability. By *not* including faculty, professional organizations, or members of the public in their deliberations, the Spellings Commission failed at bolstering commitment to their decisions and recommendations.

Taking a deliberative approach to solving higher education's myriad problems will be difficult precisely for this reason: to deliberate with others is to put oneself at great risk. One risk of deliberation "is that participants may change their minds on issues that are important to them."[24] But the same risk of deliberation is also what makes teaching so challenging. You cannot force someone to deliberate about something, or to teach something, any more than you can force students to learn something or to unlearn something; learning and deliberating are the same type of thing in that they both require *risk-taking*.

Facilitating Trust

Third, deliberation facilitates trust. The higher education leader as public advocate recognizes that issues of style and engagement about policy issues are propelled by others' emotional responses to language and social engagement. As Allen observes in her research on trust, "To provoke or assuage people's vulnerabilities is learned behavior."[25] Future leaders in higher education contexts will have to find ways to assuage stakeholder vulnerabilities—not provoke them. Being attentive to others' emotions is a behavior that can be learned. Learning and understanding more about stakeholder's vulnerabilities is also what the study and teaching of the humanities do best. Through an appreciation of aspects of human society and culture, the humanities help us gain insight into others' lives, hopes, joys, and fears. Understanding how and why some stakeholders react in certain ways to particular situations and not other situations is a kind of intelligence that is rhetorical insofar as it emphasizes observing, which is invaluable to sound leadership.[26] What is more, understanding how to respond appropriately to others' emotions is necessary for building trust with others.

Leading for the sake of higher education's public good means creating spaces and places for deliberative engagement, for people to experience higher education *as* a public good. A major benefit of such forums will likely be connecting faculty and potential leaders in advocacy efforts to wider networks that make up higher education and its external stakeholders. A deliberative approach to building capacity for leadership in higher education is important because, as large institutions, higher education already represents vast networks, often unseen, unnoticed, or inaccessible to many. In these settings, the higher education leader as public advocate helps to convene, to clarify, and to prioritize the values of the group, as well as the terms on which they collectively agree to use to judge policy.

One of the biggest challenges for leaders is to build frames that help clarify policy problems. The higher education leader as public advocate builds public frames in order to set the appropriate grounds for public argument about policy issues related to higher education (see chapter 3). For example, demonstrating accountability to the public is about demonstrating value and practicing goodwill. In summary, such advocates direct public argument to keep its public-oriented focus. In doing so, they help to structure the deliberative conditions that make democracy possible. As a result, such leaders exhibit a democratic ethic as a result of their practice, one that is committed to fairness, to demonstrating care in listening, and to supporting people as they learn to engage deliberately with others as equals. Supporting others as they learn to engage in deliberation is necessary because, as Roberts-Miller argues, "Deliberative democracy makes high demands of citizens. We must treat one another with empathy, attentiveness, and trust; we must take the time to invent and continually reinvent our ideas in the light of informed disagreement; and we must care enough about our own views to try to persuade others of them, but not so much that we are unwilling to change them; we must listen with care to people who tell us we are wrong; we must behave with grace when other views prevail; we must argue with passion but without rancor, with commitment but without intransigence."[27] Part of higher education's public promise is that it works to provide places and ways for people to practice democratic modes of deliberative engagement. We have to not only teach these forms of engagement to our students, but also model them in public ourselves.

In the remaining sections, I discuss the challenges and possibilities for faculty and graduate students to organize such deliberative forums. As future leaders in higher education, how do we cultivate conditions for others to start engaging in deliberative forms of governance? It was traditionally expected that leaders in higher education would rise through the ranks via the faculty, but as trends in administrative hiring practices have shifted more toward outsiders (in business or nonprofit management), it is imperative that we consider supporting not just faculty but also graduate students in learning to deliberate about interrelated issues affecting many of them, and their relationships to problems affecting higher education and the public in general.

Three Challenges for Leadership Training

The model for leadership that I am advocating is not without its challenges. To train current faculty, and even graduate students, for such public-facing leadership roles and to work with other public stakeholders is daunting. In this section, I explain three challenges that will likely arise in preparing faculty to undertake such roles and cultivate rhetorical practices of leadership. My hope is that addressing these challenges will help us to start finding ways that we might work from, and build from, the strengths of our faculty in institutions of higher education.

The first, and perhaps most obvious, challenge to training deliberative is that most faculty members are reluctant to engage in public-facing ways outside their area of specialization. In her conclusion to *Generous Thinking*, professor of digital humanities and media studies Kathleen Fitzpatrick admits that "I am not a community organizer; far from it. I am an academic, and a pretty introverted one at that."[28] Fitzpatrick's disclosure of vulnerability is a general fact about many (though not all) college and university faculty, one inculcated by habit and reward. Academics are generally not community organizers—they are scholars and teachers. Like many faculty members, Fitzpatrick sees herself as introverted. Many of the strengths of being introverted are precisely why people are drawn to, and succeed in, academia, where they can pursue their interests through largely independent research, or in small groups with peers or subordinate graduate students. One of the great strengths of research universities, for example, is that they allow researchers to both imagine and try out new ideas while pursuing independent, even disparate, research goals.

Part of what faculty can do as public advocates for higher education is help to strengthen others' commitment to its value by explaining and sharing what they do in ways that are meaningful to public stakeholders' shared values (see preface). For example, there is a felt need for the public to understand—from a faculty member's perspective and experience—what they do and how their work contributes to shared concerns in society. Fitzpatrick's concept of "generous thinking" is relevant here. "Generous thinking," according to Fitzpatrick, is thinking that starts from the assumption that an understanding of knowledge is not a thing one acquires, but the outcome of inquiry that requires an ongoing commitment to it. "Perhaps knowledge, and the educational systems that provide it," she observes, "are not naturally public goods; they do not spring into being freely and openly available to all, but instead require [that faculty make an] ongoing commitment and investment in order to make and keep them that way."[29] Fitzpatrick's definition of generous thinking and how to enact it publicly in rhetorical terms is akin to *epideictic* rhetoric; that is, faculty should seek to strengthen adherence to public values and recognize the need to commit to and invest in those values through doing research explicitly for the public good. This type of transformation requires a new framing for the value of higher education. For Fitzpatrick this shift in vocabulary from value to values (plural) "demands a paradigm shift" (195). Indeed, it is the *practice* of generosity—and generous thinking—that can help us cultivate a sense of trust with stakeholders external to the university.

Shifting how we talk about our research from something we value, or that has value because it is funded, to something committed to public and other stakeholder's values reveals a new way of understanding how the higher education leader is at ground a teacher and researcher, and that being a public advocate will naturally follow from this for some. For example, as teachers we already *are* public organizers. In teaching, our pedagogies are always, in some sense, a kind of public making. And even pedagogies that seem to eschew public purpose in favor of formalistic or technical knowledge are implicitly arguments for the type of public and ideal of deliberative decision-making that we value.[30]

A second challenge in training faculty for public-facing leadership is that most of us tend to be more beholden to our disciplines and disciplinary organizations than to our individual institutions of higher education in the abstract. The Spellings controversy offers a number of lessons for would-be advocates in this regard. First, the AAUP played an active public role in responding to the Commission. So there is reason to think that finding ways to participate and strengthen local chapters on campus could be a powerful way to tend to our public infrastructure in the university. It was the professional organizations in higher education such as the AAUP that provided the most important leadership by providing both counter public spaces and forums and direct connections between faculty and policymakers. A second takeaway for policymakers was that these organizations are important stakeholders in the policy efforts. The implication for faculty is that professional organizations such as the AAUP are often our best, most accessible infrastructural networks when facing public criticism. They are a great place to start practicing what public advocacy for higher education can look like, as well as important networks for creating a shared sense of our case for the public good. Finally, they also offer enclaves from which we can strengthen our sense of shared values as faculty. And most importantly, these organizations often have the resources and experience with direct efforts at lobbying.

Finally, a third challenge in training faculty for public-facing leadership is that the structure of universities encourages faculty to think and work only in enclaves. Despite the many ways that college campuses can serve as community hubs and anchors, the stereotype of the "ivory tower" persists and still accurately describes the way some faculty experience higher education inside silos. Of primary concern is the way that current trends in funding, such as performance-based budgeting and other managerial trends, encourages faculty and increasingly discrete departments to compete for resources, rather than recognize and draw strength from our interdependence.

As public educators entrusted with improving society, we have a duty to the public not only to critique the university but also to defend it, and to explain and educate others external to it about how the university actually works and for whom. As Owen-Smith argues, "Consider that many of the things students need to learn—such as how to reason and make decisions from numeric evidence, how to write effectively from that reasoning—aren't actually taught in individual departments or by specific faculty. Many of the tools that students need to pursue the projects professors assign, a single department or college doesn't provide. In this way, the units that make up a university's teaching infrastructure are *interdependent*, and their benefits can't be pinned down so specifically as to locate them in one place on campus."[31] The challenge of representing the interdependent nature of higher education has caused some leaders to shy away from doing so, but this is a mistake. Given current enthusiasm for unbundling, disrupting, or abolishing higher education institutions altogether, we need to publicly recognize and embrace the university's interconnected messiness as part of its strength rather than retreat to hyper-specialization.

Training Faculty and Students for Deliberative Public Leadership

What are some ways that we can train faculty and graduate students to undertake public-facing leadership roles and participate in deliberation about the public good with others? Most current approaches to leadership in higher education rely on either individualized mentorship or professional development via leadership institutes and workshops. But much like the literature on higher education leadership, these forms of training rely on leadership theories imported from the business world (like charismatic leadership) and other managerial techniques, and seldom provide ways of understanding the rhetorical expectations of leadership, including the ability to facilitate deliberative engagement. What is missing is guidance about how to engage public forums and ways for future leaders to practice public-facing leadership, where cultivating relationships with others is key.

The Community Think Tank Model

To provide spaces for public deliberation about higher education, I suggest we start by strengthening our local publics as a source of inspiration for enacting policy change. One successful model for cultivating local public leadership is the community think tank, taught by Linda Flower at Carnegie Mellon University in her course Leadership, Dialogue, and Change.[32] Contrary to most courses on leadership, which focus on cultivating "visionary" leaders who can persuade others to follow them, Flower's local publics model focuses on leadership as a communal practice of *public inquiry*. Grounded in John Dewey's pragmatic tradition, the community think tank model is compatible with the kind of higher education leadership I have been arguing for, insofar as it shares a commitment to the value of deliberative participation and engagement as a necessary precursor to effective policymaking.[33] It emphasizes helping others experience leadership as a form of community literacy, adaptive problem-solving, and shared inquiry. One of the most important aspects of Flower's model is that it suggests formal authority is not a requirement for exercising community leadership; it thus becomes a helpful way to train those who may not have had a formal leadership role within the university or explicit leadership training such as graduate students.

Flower's model is significant for other reasons, too, namely:

1. It offers a problem-solving approach that pays attention to shared issues and brings together diverse stakeholders.
2. It combines aspects of qualitative and social research, including critical incident interviews and practices of "rivaling" to draw out multiple perspectives.[34]
3. It embraces narrative, storytelling, and multimodal argument helpful in building a public case. In this way, it also pushes against idealized forms for deliberation and is more inclusive of a range of forms of deliberative engagement.

One upshot of this think tank model is how it draws from a rhetorical grounding to help participants see and experience the public potential of their arguments. But it also helps potential leaders learn how to write policy problem statements that draw people into a shared inquiry—not ones that provokes defensive reactions—which is one of the greatest challenges facing an advocate for higher education. Indeed, participants learn the consequences of rhetoric in public contexts. And, as in the Spellings case, they learn firsthand that how a policy problem is framed has significant effects on how people are able to debate and develop potential policy solutions for it. They learn that, if a problem is really just the responsibility or fault of one person or authority to fix, perhaps it requires a different type of advocacy altogether. For adaptive problems that require a more collective effort, such as the problems that the Spellings Commission raised about improving access and affordability of higher education, a different approach is needed to policy and governance.

Flower's community think tank can serve as a useful framework for addressing such adaptive challenges in higher education. This is because it is a scaffolded problem-solving practice of deliberation with community engagement that works across diverse stakeholders. It is also a research-oriented practice that creates usable findings, which makes it particularly well-suited for university settings and with policymakers. To start, the community think tank invites multiple stakeholders to define *a shared problem* without assuming the problem is easily perceptible or already well understood. It then provides questions and heuristics for guiding group deliberation about defining the scope of the problem, as well as options for action and outcomes. Because the framework emphasizes developing shared strategies for problem-solving, it can also be effective in cross-cultural and cross-hierarchy situations that may otherwise be stymied by top-down approaches or by "complaint and blame" sessions.[35]

ENGAGING HIGHER EDUCATION'S MANY STAKEHOLDERS

A crucial aspect of the community think tank model is how it honors the situated knowledge and expertise of a diversity of stakeholders. In higher education policy contexts, an array of internal and external stakeholders typically needs to be considered in a policy process. Internal stakeholders can include administration (varying ranks), faculty (tenure and nontenure track), clinicians, staff, hourly employees, students (undergraduate and graduate), and governing boards. External stakeholders can include taxpayers, donors, federal and state policymakers, employers in the corporate sector, union representatives (where applicable), parents of students, alumni, advisory boards, disciplinary and professional organizations, and even local community members who regularly affect or who are affected by university issues.[36]

When convening stakeholders to participate in a community think tank, leaders may consider stakeholders who can

- Help define the problem;
- Interpret the meaningfulness and significance of the problem;
- Research and extrapolate about the problem's impact at scale or over time;
- Offer an alternative perspective or experience to define its scope and significance in local, national, and global contexts;
- Develop options for action that are possible within higher education given institutional constraints;
- Have authority to enact the best option for action relevant to solving the problem(s) at the policy level;
- Evaluate whether the enacted solution has been effective in solving the problem.

Perhaps the most essential task of effective deliberative leadership is not to assemble the largest community think tank possible, or to host a town hall, but to convene a forum that has an appropriate representation of stakeholders, contribute to an understanding of a shared problem and its implications, offer productive rival interpretations of the problem, and have something at stake in the outcome of the deliberative process.

LEADING FOR THE PUBLIC GOOD 97

SCAFFOLDING PUBLIC DELIBERATION

A community think tank consists of four major parts to scaffold public deliberation: the first two parts focus on drawing in multiple stakeholder perspectives and experiences about a policy problem, while the second two parts facilitate the invention of new ideas and options for action. What's key for leaders to recognize is the way that a community think tank uses both events *and* documents to shape and mediate the deliberative process.

First, a think tank team conducts background research related to the problem and identifies key stakeholders who should be involved. A key method for doing this work is critical incident interviewing.[37] Critical incident interviews focus on documenting concrete situations and the situated knowledge of those who may affected by the problem under question. In these interviews, participants are prompted to describe specific incidents when they experienced the problem: "Can you tell me about a time when you encountered this problem . . . what happened?" The goal of the interview is to draw out and document the situated experiences that people have related to the problem. Such interviews, especially when conducted across a wide community sample, can offer rich qualitative data for documenting how the same problem might occur and affect stakeholders in different ways. Subsequently, the interview data is synthesized by the think tank team and organized into common types of scenarios where the problem occurs. These scenarios become basis for a document called a "briefing book," used in the later public discussions.

Second, an additional round of interviews (either individual or in small groups) is conducted by the think tank team to understand the causes or the "story-behind-the story" of the problem as revealed in the critical incident interviews. For example, the interviewer may ask participants, "When we interviewed others about this problem, we heard about this particular incident . . . why do you think it happened that way? What might be going on here that group X or Y may not be aware of?" The goal of these sessions is to elicit different interpretations of the problem from potentially "rival" perspectives. These rival perspectives are important because they will be used to develop a guide for further discussions when the community think tank is assembled as a whole.

Third, "decision point sessions" are assembled with larger groups—strategically bringing in stakeholders from all levels of authority. Their discussions are guided by the briefing book, which synthesizes the critical incident interview data, the "stories-behind-the-stories," and rival interpretations of a handful of key scenarios. The briefing book presents scenarios of the problem and includes question prompts that invite readers to consider multiple interpretations of the problem. Participants are guided by the briefing book and a facilitator to collaboratively generate "options for action" in response to the problems. For example, "In the first scenario, what could office X do response?" In addition, participants are prompted to describe what they anticipate the *outcomes* might be: "What might happen if office X takes that action?" Participants are invited to draw from their experiences and knowledge to map out a range of the possible consequences that might emerge from the various options for action—and to offer rival options.

Fourth, and finally, "local action think tanks" are intended to help weigh and evaluate the options for action. The community think tank leadership team documents the deliberations from the decision point sessions and the various options for action in a "findings" report that is circulated not only to participants but to the wider community. Unlike the initial briefing book, which was used as a springboard for understanding various interpretations of the problem, the findings focus more on documenting the possible actions to take and *consequences* for doing so. The audience for the findings may be a wider public or it may be those who can initiate institutional change from a different position of authority.

MODELING PUBLIC INQUIRY

What is notable about a community think tank process as a whole—in contrast to typical university modes of engagement like town hall forums, feedback sessions, or focus groups—is that it draws people into a *process of public inquiry*. The downside to such an intensive process, of course, is that it often takes a lot of time—in past community think tank cases, at least six to eighteen months. But the upshot is that people are brought into problem-solving collaboratively as respected partners, which oftentimes means they are willing to continue this work so long as it yields changes in their understanding and their lives.

At this point some readers may be wondering, does the community think tank model *actually* work? This model has been used effectively in community issues related to welfare policy, labor union negotiation, and others. This model has also been used within university settings to solve problems related to financial aid support for independent students, addressing student mental health issues, and disability advocacy.[38] In *A Responsive Rhetorical Art*, Elenore Long describes how using parts of this model (story-behind-the-story, rivaling, and critical incident) have been influential in public and institutional advocacy at Arizona State University.[39] While the community think tank may not transfer or scale seamlessly, my point is that emerging leaders in higher education need practice in adapting methods like Flower's for the purposes of modeling the public work of higher education. Such a model can be adapted for a variety of rhetorical situations where collaborative decision-making and deliberation often occur, such as university governance situations (faculty senates, college working groups, and local chapters of the AAUP, for example); city/local policy group meetings and town halls; state policy lobbying sessions and advocacy trainings; or national advocacy conferences where policy platforms are collaboratively developed and where advocacy training is provided.

Flower's model is an important one for one final reason: it offers a strong example of the importance of the humanities as a form of inquiry. Participants who learn to lead a community think tank learn unique capacities for public engagement and dialogue. They learn how to make problems a matter of shared public concern *with* members of the public, and how to navigate local complexity in ways that can be scalable to larger policy contexts.

Building a Publicly Responsive Infrastructure in Higher Education

In the years since the Spellings Commission, there has been an increased focus on how to build a stronger case for higher education's public value. Most of these efforts within higher education have focused on assessment, but they have also been about finding new ways of representing higher education's value. The work of professional organizations such as the AAC&U, for example, was key in the years following the Spellings Commission, and it will likely continue to be a source of support in the longer term. In particular, organizations such as the AAC&U have emphasized collecting data about outcomes, debt, and earnings; creating public collaboration and public-facing research; and sponsoring policy work that helps graduate students and faculty connect with representatives and policymakers. This is important work because our assumptions about assessment and the success of higher education is often so limited to quantitative assessment or outcomes defined in terms of salaries or salary-to-debt ratios.

The public advocate for higher education can contribute to strengthening public capacity building in these ways, but in others, too. One benefit to working in a university is that we can start right where we are. For example,

Flower's latest study has shown how an education in the humanities has directly shaped students' personal, social, and public lives in ways that are not captured by commonly used assessment metrics.[40] This is why it is important to begin cultivating rhetorical skills and enacting deliberative forums in our own departments, on our own campuses, or within our professional organizations. To begin building a publicly responsive infrastructure means that we start within our own enclaves, but that we also seek to find ways together to leave those enclaves and rejoin the public. Building a publicly responsive infrastructure also means that we have to embrace ways to build trust in each other and in our departments, and do much more than respond to, or interface with, the public. Good leadership requires trust. Universities are community hubs that allow the possibility for our public imagination to develop together with the public, provided we include them in our deliberations about higher education's future.

The higher education leader as public advocate is a model for how to address the very issues raised in the Spellings case. Higher education leaders need to be able to frame public issues using the public arguments for the good of the public. They need to be able to interpret value conflicts. And they need to be able to enact deliberative conditions under which decisions about problems and policy solutions are possible. When I say we need new public imaginaries for higher education, I mean we need new *practices* of collaborative inquiry. It is only by engaging people in the activity of creating public life that we can begin a process of better and beneficent policymaking for the public good.

The model of higher education leadership I have been advocating for should start by working to build a "publicly responsive infrastructure" in higher education that supports deliberation about these and other issues. Indeed, as Jennifer Clifton argues, "There is a public need within the academy for collaborative imagining, inventing, reasoning and problem solving together—the very work that is perhaps most needed for rich participation in public life. We must do more than simply recreate the structural problem of change or cannibalize disciplines and subfields or fragment into a myriad of marketing niches. Instead, this moment calls for the invention of collaborative practices and of alternative discourses, sustained over time with one another to encourage public imagination and *create a publicly responsive infrastructure*."[41] The temptation to cannibalize, cancel disciplines and subfields, or to splinter institutions into a myriad of smaller colleges, is an understandable but imprudent response to the public crisis facing higher education today. Clifton's warning about the problem of enclaving is an important one, since the desire to enclave is doubly supported by our desire to effect real change when it is repeatedly thwarted or stymied. Enclaves are understandable but myopic, and they are problematic for a deliberative model of democracy, and for democracies generally.

To go public as advocates for higher education, faculty need to tend our enclaves; and to tend our enclaves, we need to make sure that we are preparing leaders to go public. This is the work of rhetoric. As Roberts-Miller argues, "Deliberative democracy does not promote people expressing themselves from within enclaves—it requires that people try to present their own arguments in ways *that people who are very different might understand.*"[42] It is this criterion of difference, and the orientation toward audiences of others, that will be key for the higher education leader as public advocate. While the temptation to stonewall against accountability reforms is understandable, it is also important to use these policy moments as opportunities to argue for why higher education *should be* a public good.

5

A NEW RHETORIC FOR HIGHER EDUCATION ADVOCACY

The public value of universities stems from the very things that make them hard to explain and justify in terms of clear, short-term private returns.
—Jason Owen-Smith

It has been more than fifteen years since the Spellings Commission was convened in 2005, but their report remains one of the most controversial attempts at implementing broad-based higher education accountability policy in US history; it is also, arguably, one of the greatest failures in the history of US higher education policy, too. The Commission failed to engage most stakeholders in higher education productively, and it also failed to immediately implement the kinds of measures that Margaret Spellings hoped to enact during the reauthorization of the subsequent Higher Education Act. However, this did not mean the Commission's report lacked long-term impact. To the contrary, as a result of the public controversy it created, the Commission solidified a rhetoric of accountability for evaluating colleges and universities, a managerial style for policymaking increasingly adopted by policymakers and higher education leadership, and a sense of crisis about the public's responsiveness to higher education's perceived "value" that continues to dominate the policymaking landscape today.

To give one example of the Spellings Commission's continued influence, the measures the Commission recommended regarding data collection and transparency were a forerunner to the College Scorecard, launched in 2015 and updated in 2022, as well as to changes in assessment measures as part of college and university accreditation.[1] The Spellings Commission also brought into stark relief the consumer-based model for representing the value of higher education outcomes we live with today, through various schemes to measure and report about colleges and universities. Ironically, it remains unclear whether such databases or websites such as the College Scorecard and now others will have any impact on how students select where they go to school. The tangible result of efforts such as the College Scorecard that Spellings recommended are the vast databases of institutional, and soon student, data. Unfortunately, figuring out what to do with all that data, or interpreting what it means, is not particularly intuitive or useful for most students and parents, or for that matter even for those who study higher education.

While the Spellings Commission report framed students and parents as information-hungry bargain hunters in search of maximum value for their education dollar, it has also yet to be shown whether this kind of information actually saves parents or students money, or if it changes how students decide where to attend college in the first place. Evidence points to the contrary. For instance, a 2016 study by the American Council on Education (ACE) and the Center for Policy Research and Strategy found that the most important factor in determining where a student chooses to go to college is not its perceived value, cost, or return on investment but its geographical location and proximity to home.[2]

A lack of public deliberation about what constitutes value for the public, let alone a "good value," poses long-term problems for higher education. So does the belief that the public or policymakers could discover the value of an education judgment-free by measuring, surveying, or cataloging institutional data about college, university, and student performance. As Jeffrey Muller explains, measuring things is not an alternative to judging them; measurement *demands* judgment: judgment about whether to measure something or not, what to measure, how to evaluate the significance of what's been measured, whether rewards and penalties will be attached to the results of such measurements, and to whom to make the measurements available to all matter, and are all a matter of judgment.[3] It is increasingly clear how much faculty expertise is needed to help shape such measures, to help judge what can and cannot be measured in higher education contexts, how to measure it, whether it should be measured in the first place, and to deliberate about the limits of measurement in public policymaking decisions concerning higher education.

I do not think this burden is fair for faculty, but I do think it's *necessary* since both faculty and their institutions are no longer publicly perceived as accurate judges of a student's success, and because we have become increasingly reactive to policies rather than proactive in resisting, questioning, and deliberating about what they should be.

I am certainly not the first person to argue that those of us in higher education, especially faculty, should be more proactive in shaping higher education public policy. David Ward—former president of the American Council on Education (ACE), and the only member of the Spellings Commission who refused to sign its final report—remarked in a reflection about his experience on the commission that "our future cannot be left to reluctant and reactive responses to public policies but must also be proactive outcome of our own creative aspirations."[4] But in fact, that has been our future, and most colleges and universities today spend an exorbitant amount of time, money, and other human resources being reactive in response to public policies related to assessment and accountability. In part, it has been our "inability to articulate the value of higher education," as Luke Winslow argues, and to engage with external stakeholders that has left us playing defense rather than working proactively to shape higher education's public aspirations.[5] The Spellings case is an example of why many of us in higher education need to better engage in policymaking collaboratively with policymakers, and the need to be engaging each other in our deliberations *about higher education's democratic purpose.*[6]

As public educators, we have a duty to the public not only to defend our colleges and universities but also to deliberate, explain, and educate other stakeholders about how such institutions really work. This is not going to be an easy task. But the need to do so is particularly urgent, given the persistent hype around unbundling, disrupting, or abolishing public higher education. Faculty and administrative higher education leadership need to recognize and embrace that the multiple missions and interdependent parts of our universities are part of higher education's strength, not its liability. Universities have lots of missions, and there are many ways they already provide for the public good. So it isn't necessarily an issue of finding the "right mission" or message for higher education so much as it is discerning what to prioritize, in what situations, for which audiences, and when.

Getting clear about our shared (and not shared) public imaginaries for higher education's value and engaging leaders in the university as its wisest public advocates is important because how we understand the public values of higher education changes how we assess and hold it and each other accountable to ourselves and others. And assessing the "value" of higher education and how to account for it is the biggest issue in higher education policy right now. That is why this book focuses on how we should deliberate about making higher education a better good for the public, and it has turned to rhetorical theory to help us begin developing capacities for a new rhetoric of higher education.

What We Have Learned About Public Leadership

This book set out to address three questions that higher education advocates face today:

1. How can we make a case for policymakers to uphold higher education's public promise?
2. What is the best way to measure and represent higher education's value as a public good?
3. How can institutions of higher education help prepare leaders with the rhetorical capabilities needed for effective public advocacy?

In offering one set of answers to these three questions, I have argued that we need to make stronger cases to policymakers about upholding higher education's public promise, but that such cases are stymied by poor historical models and two interrelated issues: first, the dominance of the managerial style in higher education policymaking and leadership has created a rhetorical framework that narrowly circumscribed how we can talk about the public good and higher education (chapter 1); and second, the language of the marketplace and its emphasis on efficiency, transparency, and accountability has created situations in which accountability to the public is really a kind of accountability to individuals in a competitive economic marketplace rather than to the collective good of a democratic public (chapter 2). Therefore, finding ways to best measure and represent higher education's value as a public good is constrained because the "value" of education is increasingly defined solely in terms of what's measurable, including such things as an individual's postgraduation income earnings or a college's completion rates.

Ultimately, our very narrow framework for imagining accountability has also meant that we lack a shared set of commonplaces (with policymakers, the public, and other stakeholders) to help springboard ways for making higher education better align with the values we share rather than strictly business or partisan values (chapter 3). To train leaders with the rhetorical capabilities needed for more effective public advocacy, I argued for a deliberative model of leadership that values public advocacy work and the reciprocal role that universities play in shaping our sense of public purpose (chapter 4).

In the remainder of this chapter, I address two contemporary policy issues that exemplify why we need leaders to be public advocates for higher education, now more than ever.

The College Scorecard and the Traps of Transparency

On September 12, 2015, the Obama administration unveiled the College Scorecard.[7] An online Web app, the College Scorecard keeps a running "score" comparing the costs, graduation rates, employment rates, average federal loan amounts borrowed by students, and loan default rates of students at every US college and university. Designed to give college-bound students, their parents or guardians, and policymakers ways to compare and contrast schools, the Department of Education's data-driven initiative was buoyed by hopes that it would make information about higher education more transparent for all—and therefore presumably more equitable—while holding institutions of higher education "accountable" for the quality of education they were providing to students. Eight years after the Spellings Commission ended their work, the College Scorecard emerged as the first version of their proposed "consumer-friendly" database.

Almost immediately, however, many policy analysts and educators criticized the College Scorecard because its metrics for keeping score seemed to narrowly define higher education quality and thus its value. In many ways, the subsequent debate about the Scorecard mirrored the controversy over the Spellings Report. Of primary concern was that the Scorecard was fundamentally a technical solution to the complex social problems of access and equity in higher education. For example, some critics argued that the Scorecard was a strictly market-based solution to education accountability reform and that, far from fixing inequity, it merely kept track of it.[8]

Additionally, other critics argued the Scorecard offered little to no help for interpreting and comparing the data it presented, while still others argued that not only was the Scorecard not transparent, but it was also distortive. For example, National Public Radio (NPR) Senior Education Editor Cory Turner reported that "the federal government has backed a dump truck [of data] to consumers' doors and left it to students and their parents to compare all those apples and oranges."[9] At its best, its critics argued, the Scorecard would simply overwhelm students and their parents or guardians. At its worst, the Scorecard would mislead people into believing that the Department of Education could provide the most relevant information needed to evaluate and compare college quality, or a school's fair market value (the price at which an asset sells in a competitive auction setting).

The controversy surrounding the Scorecard illuminates a continued pressing issue for college leaders and educators today: calls for education reform and accountability continue to be dominated by the values and ideals of the market. Students and their parents or guardians continue to be positioned as consumers shopping in an education marketplace for a good deal for themselves, rather than as citizens participating in improving the public good.

In the near term, the College Scorecard could have a major impact on higher education accountability as part of the recent College Transparency Act (HR 2030), part of the America COMPETES Act of 2022 (HR 4521) and sponsored by Senators Elizabeth Warren and Orrin Hatch. Its bipartisan mission vastly expands our federal postsecondary data infrastructure by overturning the federal ban on student-level data collection in the Higher Education Act of 2007/8, with the stated goals of evaluating student enrollment patterns, progression, completion, and postcollegiate outcomes and higher education costs and financial aid.

Its "user-friendly site" will provide much more information for students and families making decisions about postsecondary education, and reduce the requirements for reporting by institutions of higher education by allowing "student-level data to be periodically matched with other federal systems of data."[10] President of the Institute for Higher Education Policy (IHEP) Mamie Voight argues that such infrastructure is needed because "students deserve to know which institutions will provide them with the best return on investment. Policymakers should be equipped to target resources to promote student success and scale effective interventions. And institutions and employers should be able to enhance opportunities to build a stronger, more dynamic workforce."[11]

The College Transparency Act—and the federal ban on student-level data collection it overturns—are related to the Spellings Commission and its failure to implement its policy recommendations in important but counterintuitive ways. For example, following the release of the Commission's report in 2007, critics in higher education and professional organizations pressured legislatures to create provisions in the reauthorization of the

Higher Education Acts that explicitly prevented the federal government from collecting data on student-level performance the report encouraged.

Contra Spellings's recommendation, the measures to prevent, rather than authorize, student-level data collection were enacted with help from Congress in 2008, most notably by then-Senator Lamar Alexander, a Republican from Tennessee. Alexander became an important and influential critic in the Spellings case because of his background as the former president of the University of Tennessee, and because he was the U.S. Secretary of the Department of Education from 1991 to 1993. Alexander's part in Congress during the Spellings controversy was important since he had the opportunity to testify before the Commission before the final report was drafted, and then again after the report was released in preparation for the 2007/8 reauthorization of the *Higher Education Act* (HEA), which continued federal funding for higher education.

In various speeches and testimonies, beginning in 2005 before the release of the final Spellings Report, Alexander called attention to the "global crisis" described in the report, which he saw as the loss of the country's "brainpower advantage": "Aside from the war on terror, there is no greater challenge than maintaining our brainpower advantage so we can keep our good-paying jobs. That is the surest way to keep America on top."[12] According to Alexander, "The greatest threat to the quality of American higher education is not underfunding. It is overregulation."[13] He urged the Spellings Commission to "join [him] on the bandwagon for deregulation of higher education."[14] However, the recommendations of the final Spellings Report ended up being very far afield of Alexander's call.

Following the release of the Spellings Report, whole institutions and educational organizations scrambled to either jump on the "voluntary accountability" measures bandwagon or to help build a stone wall against accountability. Alexander worked quickly to create an alliance of those who opposed any additions to the HEA that tied federal funding to standardized accountability measures and sought to limit access to the student-level data they would be measured against. In a Senate hearing on the reauthorization of the HEA in May 2007, Alexander summed up the problem with accountability for higher education, and his problem with the Commission, by putting his audience in the position of having to deny the importance of free-market choice if they voted to approve the recommendations of the Spellings Commission: "The question is whether you believe that excellence in higher education comes from institutional autonomy, markets, competition, choice for students, federalism, and limited Federal regulation . . . or whether you don't."[15] In a strange, yet perhaps not unexpected, twist in the accountability debate, Alexander argued *against* the accountability measures supported by the Spellings Commission by describing the "free-marketplace" being free of regulations.

Unlike advocates who argued against the Spellings recommendations on the grounds that higher education should not be treated as a business and therefore should be held accountable to its investors and shareholders, Alexander argued against them on the grounds that higher education should be treated like a free market and therefore free of proposed accountability measures (regulations). Alexander instead proposed that Congress enact a three-part solution for accountability:

1. Aggressive "jawboning": "First, convene leaders in higher education... and let them know in clear terms that if colleges and universities do not accept more responsibility for assessment and accountability, the Federal Government will do it for them."
2. Competition through incentives: "Second, establish an award for accountability in higher education."
3. Development grants for outside researchers: "[Three,] make research and development grants to states, institutions, accreditors and assessment researchers to develop new and better appropriate measures of accountability."

What is significant about Alexander's testimony is that he presumed to share the ends of many higher education advocates who were antiaccountability but had much different values and different means to achieve them. Alexander also employed similarly dissociative strategies to push for a vision of education inconsistent with the ideals of many (though not all) in higher education who were also critical of Spellings. His influential position and background meant that his discourses were often the most circulated and impactful in shaping the reauthorization of the HEA, helping to add and influence policy provisions that ultimately limited the power of the Department of Education, including limitations on student-level data collection.

Furious with the provisions that Alexander was able to secure for the HEA, in February 2008 Margaret Spellings wrote an article that appeared in *Politico* entitled "Congress Digs a Moat Around Its Ivory Tower,"[16] in which she argued that "while business leaders embrace the future, Congress is vigorously defending old structures and outdated practices in higher education at the behest of entrenched stakeholders who advocate that status quo."

Associating her Commission's work with business and the future, and aligning higher education with the past, Spellings made the case that higher education had secured an unprecedented form of exceptionalism.

The public debate between Spellings and Alexander is significant in the history of education policymaking not so much because of accountability per se, but because it demonstrates competing ideals of business and "the marketplace" itself. While Spellings saw higher education as a business that needed to be better regulated and managed with standardized mechanisms for maximum efficiency, Alexander positioned higher education as a "marketplace of 6,000 autonomous institutions" that needed less regulation for maximum efficiency. In short, their disagreement boiled down to one of market regulation, and by analogy to a disagreement about the appropriate scope of the federal government in higher education's affairs.

Though Alexander was cited at the time as a major ally for higher education in fending off a potentially problematic set of accountability measures and metrics from becoming federally mandated, his public speeches set a problematic precedent for education policy by strengthening a suspicious attitude toward federal power in higher education reform, while further associating the values of higher education with free-market values. At a time when public funding for higher education is *decreasing*, strengthening the connection between higher education's public purpose and the government is key for continued funding.

Alexander's speeches also associated an antiaccountability position with the values of free choice, markets, and competition. In doing so, Alexander actually reinforced many aspects of the prevailing free-market ideology that characterized much of the Commission's initiatives—and subsequent criticism—in the first place. As Emily Toth argued in an article published in *Inside Higher Ed* at the time, "The irony of these periodic bursts of regulatory enthusiasm is that the conservative, free-market political enterprise appears most eager to see this educational free market socialized into government mandated homogeneity, often based on simple, one dimensional measures."[17] The supposed "irony" here that Toth refers to can be understood when examined through the lens of the managerial style (chapter 1)—a style that functions to resolve paradoxes of values by making a particular economic rationality a reality.[18]

The College Transparency Act of 2022 brings the same issues back into focus again, since, like almost all the policies proposed for data collection, it is bipartisan. And those in higher education now face many of the same issues as their colleagues did with the Spellings Commission fifteen years ago: the enthusiasm for metrics and accountability remains a bipartisan issue with few detractors, and even many professional organizations seem happy to sign on to it in the name of "transparency." One problem here is that making all this data available and "public" does not guarantee that its meaning will be transparent, and in fact it will be very hard to *interpret* or make sense of it all. This criticism is one raised by critics in the Spellings case. Recent arguments against the College Scorecard, and to a lesser degree the College Transparency Act, use the same starting places for their arguments against it as did opponents of the Spellings Report then, including:

- *Privacy*: Right to student privacy.
- *Waste*: Wasted effort; the money, time, and human resources spent on data collection and interpretation could be used better to educate students than track them.
- *Fairness*: Rules enforced inconsistently for different types of institutions.
- *Autonomy*: Suspicion about how the federal government will use the data. Also concern about government overreach, since policymakers should not get to decide what programs are funded, influence what majors students should pursue, etc.

Additionally, many critics of the College Transparency Act argue that the Department of Education's job should not be to regulate the higher education marketplace or crack down on institutions with "unacceptable" outcomes. The challenge is that making such data widely available, while expanding the Department of Education's regulatory power based on that information, can sometimes be blurred in the rhetoric of such debates. In other words, institutions of higher education know that calls to report more information are never neutral—they are almost always attempts to regulate, control, and ultimately punish schools that are not meeting standards.

The continued emphasis on data transparency in higher education, often framed as a prerequisite for "accountability" in general, is an admirable condition to aspire to, but also a potential trap. In our aspirations for total transparency, we rely on the false assumption that all knowledge is knowable in the same way, and that anything we could know about can always be represented in the numerical forms we have constructed within such systems. In short, the term "transparency" functions in policy debates about higher education as a building block that is a summary of an attitude or an ideology about the value of what we already think we know—and how we think we can know it—than an actually achievable goal of knowing the full worth of a student's education or working to improve on it.

Many of the issues higher education will continue to face surrounding data transparency, especially transparency of student-level data under the College Transparency Act, are yet another reminder that both higher education and the public need to better confront problems of value and address conflicts about data, transparency, and knowledge. In particular, I think the humanistic disciplines bear special responsibility, since it is part of our job to equip others with ways to analyze value-laden propositions, for giving perspective on the value assumptions of our own culture, and for providing an understanding of how that data-driven culture evolved. We also offer some exposure to history and cultures remote from ours in time and space, and for helping others to experience works of imaginative literature and creative nonfiction in which such questions of value are inescapable.

The Gates Commission and the Question of Value

In addition to the Scorecard, and now the College Transparency Act, the lasting impact of the Spellings Report and the controversy surrounding it can also be seen in recent work by the Bill and Melinda Gates Foundation's Postsecondary Value Commission. Responding to concerns that the Spellings Commission was too narrowly focused on measuring student learning as means for verifying higher education's economic benefit—and not more broadly focused on how such benefits relate to issues of social and economic equity across gender and racial categories—the Gates Commission framed its mission as one about equity. While it is clear that the Gates Commission framed itself as much different from the Spellings Commission, what is less clear is how the tools they propose to determine and report on higher education's value will make a more just society.

Sponsored by the Gates Foundation but managed by the Institute for Higher Education Policy (IHEP), and cochaired by Mildred Garcia, president of the American Association of State College and Universities (AASCU), the Commission included thirty members from across higher education institutions and organizations.[19] It began its work in 2019 and was charged with determining the question "What is a college degree worth?" To answer it, the Commission used the federal College Scorecard and public data provided the University of Texas System, which they describe as "a vanguard on the use of postsecondary data to understand and promote student success" to determine how students "experience value."[20] But in addition to determining market value and creating a metric system of "thresholds," the Commission was also guided by another aim: *equity*.

To some extent, this mission of the Gates Commission could be interpreted as a much-needed improvement from aspects of the Spellings Commission in a number of ways. First, it draws from a wider range of higher education experts and focuses on the issue of *value*, which so clearly became a public point of contention in the Spellings case. And second, it is much more attentive to issues of race, gender, and equity in higher education.

However, despite these improvements, the Gates Commission, with its emphasis on economic return on investment, shares many of the problems of the Spellings Commission. First and foremost, it fundamentally prioritizes economic returns for individual students as the defining characteristic of higher education's value. For example, the Commission cites as its greatest contribution to policymaking a new definition of value that accounts for different six different vectors or "thresholds":

1. Minimum economic return: A student meets this threshold if they earn *at least* as much as a comparable high school graduate, plus enough to recoup their total net price for the degree plus interest within ten years.
2. Earnings premium: A student meets this threshold if they reach at least median earnings in their field of study (or, if field of study data is unavailable, the median earnings for the institution's predominant degree type).
3. Earnings parity: A student meets this threshold in terms of whether they are students of color, students from low-income backgrounds, and women who reach the median earnings of their systemically more advantaged peers (e.g., white, high-income, or male).
4. Economic mobility: A student meets this threshold if they reach the level of earnings to enter into the fourth (60th to 80th percentile) income quintile, regardless of their field of study.
5. Economic security: A student meets this threshold if they reach median levels of wealth (e.g., retirement, savings, etc.).
6. Wealth parity: A student meets this threshold as a student of color, a student from a low-income background, or a woman student who reaches the level of wealth (e.g., retirement, savings, etc.) attained by their more systematically advantaged peers (e.g., white, high-income, or male).[21]

While such thresholds are worthy aims to help disadvantaged students achieve, the website offers little advice on how such thresholds ought to be better met. What is more, the Commission's final report seems to suggest that racism and sexism are primarily the result of economic inequity, not its causes. The report appears to try to account for forms of social inequity in the United States as a result of higher education, rather than as part of social and political issues in which higher education is only a part. It is common to frame higher education as both cause and cure for society's ills. As Labaree explains, "Higher ed is now in the crosshairs of educational policy reformers, since it has evolved into the central educational institution for allocating social opportunity and social advantage. It's in the uncomfortable position occupied by the high school for most of the twentieth century, and as a result it's the natural target for our worst fears and greatest aspirations."[22] The central irony around higher education's supposed "declining value" comes about precisely because higher education offers so many advantages to any student and is already obviously valuable. But policymakers also err in ascribing *too* much power to higher education in their expectation that it can fix broader social and political problems.

Unfortunately, the types of conclusions that we can draw from these data-collection efforts are limited. For example, the Gates Commission draws most of its conclusions about the value of higher education from the same publicly available College Scorecard data, data that is simultaneously both vast and quite limited because it only includes data about students in general who received *federal* aid. There should be an additional concern that their effort to amass such information (often delivered without much context, save a warning that it offers no context) also leaves colleges and universities vulnerable to (sometimes) undeserved criticism along racial and gender lines—and a degree of luck—in how they're compared and ranked by the commission in terms of their ability to manufacture what the commission has equated to "social equity." For their part, the Commission seems somewhat aware of these concerns, since there are three reminders on their website that pop up when viewers use the "Value Equity Explorer," a tool created for students, parents, and policymakers. They warn that "context matters—While assessing institutional performance, users must consider an institution's context, including the institutional mission, state policy and financial support, local and regional labor market conditions, and history." And while it is useful for the Commission to acknowledge the importance of context, it should also be concerning when we consider how challenging it is to know things like "context." For example, who can—or who will—provide that context? In addition to the issue of context, they also acknowledge that "the data are incomplete—This tool leverages the best available public data, but those data are incomplete, so results should be interpreted with great caution." The warning about the "incompleteness" of the data and for proceeding with caution generally seems wise. But then, how can users of the site reasonably make sense of incomplete or missing data? What data, after all, is not there, and what aspects of an education could never be there? "The data tool displays outcomes but does not diagnose causes— Due to data limitations, and the complexity of measuring postsecondary value, this data tool and the underlying data are designed to inform institutional improvement efforts, not to develop institutional rankings, penalize institutions, or make causal claims about value."[23] Their third warning addresses many of the concerns that have been raised by higher education officials, especially about the way that standardized performance metrics may be used to penalize institutions. However, it seems shortsighted to think that data collected and represented in this way would *not* invite causal claims about value, whether one adds a warning label to it or not. In acknowledging that the tool is designed to inform institutional improvement efforts, we might wonder: is this tool, especially when its productive uses are actively and necessarily discouraged, truly the best way to do that?

Finally, and perhaps most disappointing, while the site gives higher education a way to say that a higher education degree is still "worth it" in terms of overall earnings compared to people without a college degree along racial and gender lines, it does not report much information that is particularly new or surprising. Instead, the Commission affirms what we already know through other means about how students of historically underrepresented groups are at a disadvantage when it comes to higher education and in the United States more generally. It reminds us that Harvard has only 11 percent Pell Grant recipients, while the nearby community college has 48 percent. Such data points may, in some cases, be useful, but it is unclear whether they are needed to reaffirm what we already know. In some respects, the Commission's work might be thought admirable and an important contribution to our understanding of the ways in which institutions of higher education play a powerful role in furthering the economic disparities of its graduates, yet it lacks any historical context for the numbers it reports.

We need alternative ways for deliberating about value, and *values*, of conceptualizing the public good and understanding the significance of higher education for promoting social equity beyond its market-based function. While I commend the Gates Commission for making much-needed changes in how higher education policy talks about "value" in terms of issues of equity, I think what is needed in terms of public leadership for higher education is shared deliberation about what its value should be.

The Hidden Dangers of Metric Fixation

While the Gates Commission argues that their mission of determining the value of higher education is accomplished by simply collecting, collating, and sharing publicly available data about colleges and universities—albeit with warning labels—the seeming innocuousness of their work could have significant dangers and likely consequences down the line. For example, it is always going to be difficult to separate the collecting of student-level data—should the College Transparency Act be put into law—from the likelihood that it will also *not* be used to assess, compare, and punish some institutions at the same time it will reward others. While student-level data may not seem particularly controversial on its own, it is important to be wary of eleven unintended but predictable negative consequences when relying on aggregated metrics to evaluate or motivate the improvement of higher education:[24]

1. Goal displacement through diversion of effort to what gets measured;
2. Promoting short-termism;
3. Costs in employee time;
4. Diminishing utility;
5. Rule cascades;
6. Rewarding luck;
7. Discouraging risk-taking;
8. Discouraging innovation;
9. Discouraging cooperation and common purpose;
10. Degradation of work;
11. Cost to productivity.

These eleven potential dangers for higher education due to a more robust postsecondary data infrastructure should serve as a useful set of reminders for advocates and higher education leadership to consider how to, or to deliberate whether or not to, implement such metrics in the first place; and, if so, how they ought to be interpreted and constrained. In the case of the Gates Commission, I think we should be reasonably concerned about at least four of these potential outcomes: goal displacement, discouraging risk-taking, discouraging cooperation and common purpose, and degradation of work.

First, there should be concern about goal displacement through the diversion of higher education's efforts toward what gets measured, rather than toward what we want as an outcome. Second, there is the fact that purely metric-based evaluation may discourage intellectual and inquiry-based risk-taking necessary for the innovation higher education likes to claim. Thus, rather than experiment or try out new things, most institutions will be incentivized to provide cover. Third, we should be concerned that such efforts discourage cooperation and common purpose. For example, the entire data infrastructure has been set up to compare and contrast colleges along narrow valuations, instead of also accounting for the common goals and ways in which colleges and universities operate in concert—or by mirroring one another's efforts—rather than autonomously. Fourth, there should be concern about the degradation of work. Ultimately, the danger is that we will spend more time trying to look like we have achieved something according to a certain metric or set of them, but without doing the actual work or imagining new ways such work might be done.

Any time we are working with people or in a profession that deals primarily with people (like higher education), we need to pay careful attention to how performance metrics are introduced as a way to shape judgments about the institution. Metrics can inform judgment, but they cannot themselves "make decisions" for us. My concern is that our tendency to gravitate toward metrics is an avoidance tactic in higher education, especially when we have need for the kind of knowledge and wisdom that can only be gained through experience (*phronesis* or prudence). Indeed, one of the more concerning statements made about the Postsecondary Value Commission report is that it can help colleges and universities make tough decisions. It's not clear how it would, and if anything, it introduces new conceptual problems of sense-making.

But at a time when understanding and implementing "data-driven decision-making" is considered a key job requirement for senior university leadership, we might start to wonder: is there any way to work in higher education *without* dealing with performance metrics? As Muller explains: "While we are bound to live in an age of measurement, we live in an age of mismeasurement, overmeasurement, misleading measurement, and counter-productive measurement. . . . The problem is not measurement, but excessive measurement and inappropriate measurement—not metrics, but metric fixation."[25] I share Muller's belief that the problem is perhaps not with metrics, but with a kind of fixation on metrics as an inappropriate and inadequate replacement for *good judgment*. For example, at a public roundtable in 2012, Judith Butler similarly framed the problem not necessarily as a problem of metrics themselves, but the fact that there has been such a narrowing of what constitutes those metrics in terms of the quantifiable: "There was a time when we talked about poetic measure or metrics, or about a measure as an important part of Aristotelian ethics. . . . You know, there is a measure for measure. We have to figure out a measure for measure."[26] In referencing the importance of measure for Aristotle's normative ethics, Butler draws our attention to the way that measurement and evaluation are not in themselves wrong or problematic: "Although we are also seeing a new and increasing demand to establish the profitability of disciplines, we are also seeing a new regime of values that certainly includes profitability as one component, but which includes as well 'impact,' marketable skills, managerial efficiency, donor appeal, the appreciation of human capital, and the internal demands of systems analysis, all of which have been identified as hallmarks of neoliberalism. This set of values requires closer scrutiny as much for what it includes as for what it effaces and even pushes toward oblivion."[27] Here Butler refers to what I have called "managerial style" (chapter 1). What is important about their observation is that such a style is not just about establishing the marketplace and profitability as its aim, but also about displacing academic and humanistic values with managerial ones (efficiency, human capital, and systems).

Like Butler and Muller, we should share in a commitment to helping institutions of higher learning make better, wiser decisions for the whole. My concern is that in our attempt to measure value, we may be misled by the allure of metrics in a way that works against our better judgment as educators. The role of higher education advocates is to help enact better, wiser judgments with a wider plurality of stakeholders. Such advocates should help advise on how much weight to give to metrics, recognize their characteristic distortions, and distinguish and argue persuasively for what cannot be measured. This is the *rhetorical* expertise that higher education's faculty bring to the practice of wise policymaking.

The Need for a New Rhetoric

In *The New Rhetoric*, Chaïm Perelman and Lucie Olbrechts-Tyteca found inspiration in the classical rhetorical tradition for developing a new rhetoric—a theoretical framework for public argumentation that would help people argue more deliberatively and to grapple collectively with the uncertainty that permeates our shared public life. Most importantly, their commitment to justice and to the rebuilding of a global movement for reconciliation following the world wars offers a kind of guide for resolving shared problems for which there is no clear answer.

In parallel fashion, the goal of this much shorter book has been to help those in higher education consider how a rhetorical approach can help us begin identifying and better arguing against the market frame and managerialism, and for enacting spaces for public deliberation about shared problems for which there is no clear answer. Another goal of this book has been to offer a perspective on how taking a rhetorical approach to higher education leadership might help reorient ways of policy engagement for higher education. To do so, I have organized this book in a way that is similar to *The New Rhetoric*, with its emphasis on the argument starting places (*topoi* or *loci communes*) for both *producing* and *understanding* arguments about higher education. At the same time, I have also tried to model the spirit of their work—to the extent that a spirit can be modeled—in that I am arguing that changes in higher education will require a new rhetoric, one that can only come into being through the activity of making public arguments and through the practices of communal leadership.

A key part of Perelman and Olbrechts-Tyteca's contribution to contemporary rhetorical theory was to reinvigorate the concept of *epideictic* rhetoric, that form of ceremonial rhetoric focused on either praise or blame. This kind of rhetoric has had an important relationship to education. By working to articulate and then strengthening adherence to a community's shared values, the epideictic orator necessarily turns *educator*. Put another way, educators are society's greatest exemplars of *epideictic* rhetoric because they are expected to uphold and continually reinforce the shared values of a society.

In a democracy, the role of the educator is to strengthen adherence to democratic values, and most debates about higher education policy are fundamentally debates about the role of higher education in a democracy. They are debates about higher education's purpose, whom they serve, what they teach, how they teach it, and for whom.

In an era of increased scrutiny of both democracy and accountability, higher education is dominated by partisan political ideals and the ideals of the marketplace, metric fixation, and a style of public engagement that prioritizes appeals to self-interest over society. We need an alternative approach for deliberative leadership engagement with policymakers, each other, and the rest of society about the ends of public higher education and its relationship to democracy. Making the effort to argue for higher education as a public good and to defend it as such, while seeking imaginative ways to strengthen our interdependent and interconnected strengths is crucial. Instead of asking, How many? when considering policy actions—especially something that will require us to spend enormous amounts of time and energy—we would do better to deliberate the following of a given policy proposal:

1. Does the policy encourage us to do better in reaching our public aims? Or does it use shame and embarrassment to encourage individuals or institutions to game the system?
2. Does the policy encourage us to act collectively to address shared problems? Or does it put people and institutions in competition with one another?
3. Does the policy share burden equitably?
4. Is the policy wise?

The most important way to shape such a policy will not come about by finding the correct arguments, or the best solution, but in adapting models for ongoing deliberative engagement that help illuminate our shared public challenges and the possibilities for public higher education in this and the next century. Since it is unlikely that current policymakers will change the course of higher education policy without motivation, those of us in higher education will have to lead the way. This book has been one attempt at helping us to better advocate for that public promise.

EPILOGUE

I began work on this book before the global COVID-19 pandemic, which has profoundly impacted institutions of higher education. As many have already observed, the pandemic exacerbated existing social, economic, and accessibility inequities. It also revealed that the "value" of higher education for many is much more than a credential one could earn online. At the same time, the pandemic demonstrated both the need for colleges and universities to participate more fully in our public infrastructure and the degree to which they already do. Higher education's ability to respond to shared public problems such as the COVID-19 pandemic—especially problems we cannot fully anticipate or easily solve—requires that its leaders strengthen their publicly responsive infrastructure by focusing on higher education's public mission and reimagining its future.

In reflecting on the COVID-19 pandemic while teaching and researching in a public university, I am reminded of the prescient metaphors that Jason Owen-Smith used in his book *Research Universities for the Public Good*.[1] Owen-Smith describes how universities play an essential role in our society through three metaphors: networks, hubs, and communities. Though Owen-Smith focuses specifically on the US research university, metaphors that emphasize interconnectedness apply well to other institutional forms, from state to community colleges and between liberal arts schools and art institutes. Our colleges and universities create powerful *networks* that bring together various forms of expertise and experience for the purpose of creating knowledge. They also create *hubs* of knowledge in communities and across *communities* for addressing urgent and nonurgent, but potentially catastrophic, problems. While many problems in higher education have economic impact and promise for market innovation, many do not. This is as it should be because the primary purpose of the university is not to create monetary profit for some, or for itself, but to create knowledge for the sake of all. We must be absolutely clear about this primary purpose in everything we do in higher education as teachers and researchers.

The metaphors of networks, hubs, and communities help to make vivid the significance of higher education in responding to the COVID-19 pandemic. From the beginning of the pandemic, researchers such as aerosol scientist Linsey Marr were arguing that the virus was airborne. What is notable is that Marr did not start her research in response to the pandemic—she had been studying aerosol transmission for years. When higher education institutions enact their potential for public infrastructure—even when working on problems that do not seem readily apparent—they are often developing solutions to problems the public may care deeply about long in advance.

Marr's example of research for the public good illuminates Owen-Smith's metaphors of the university. The university—as much more than the sum of its parts—is also a powerful network that can bring together various forms of expertise and experience quickly for the purpose of creating knowledge for the public good. At the same time, universities connect communities of researchers and people from across the United States and globally. And, unlike pharmaceutical companies, which by their nature seek to monetize research for profit, researchers and teachers at our public universities seek to generally benefit the public welfare.

This example of Marr's research is one of the many ways that higher education plays an inextricable role in contributing to the public good already. At the same time, it is indicative of its potential to better fulfill its promise when leadership is committed to advocating for their public mission in policy cases. There is much about the pandemic that has harmed and strained the bonds of trust between citizens and government institutions, including higher education. But trust is not a static thing; it is created and strengthened through consistent engagement. As Thomas Goodnight reminds us, "The full worth of a policy is always yet to be seen. Argumentation offers a momentary pause in the flow of events, an opportunity to look down the present road as well as paths untaken. As deliberation raises expectations that are feared or hoped for, public argument is a way to share in the construction of the future."[2] We cannot know or predict the future, but through deliberative work, we can prepare for what may be ahead.

Higher education is modern society's way of building a publicly responsive infrastructure. While the global pandemic may have revealed some of our greatest weaknesses, it also reminds us why we must continue to take care of our institutions, and to cultivate and train leaders who are as committed and attuned to deliberating about issues of social justice and equity as they are about the technical aspects of running a college.[3]

APPENDIX: MEMBERS OF THE COMMISSION
ON THE FUTURE OF HIGHER EDUCATION
(ALSO KNOWN AS THE SPELLINGS COMMISSION)

Charles Miller (Chairman), Private Investor, Former Chairman of the Board of Regents, University of Texas System

Nicholas Donofrio, Executive Vice President, Innovation and Technology, IBM Corporation

James J. Duderstadt, President Emeritus, University Professor of Science and Engineering; Director, the Millennium Project, University of Michigan

Gerri Elliott, Corporate Vice President, Worldwide Public Sector, Microsoft Corporation

Jonathan N. Grayer, Chairman and CEO, Kaplan, Inc.

Kati Haycock, Director, the Education Trust

James B. Hunt Jr., Chairman, Hunt Institute for Educational Policy and Leadership; former Governor of North Carolina

Arturo Madrid, Murchison Distinguished Professor of Humanities, Department of Modern Languages and Literatures, Trinity University

Robert Mendenhall, President, Western Governors University

Charlene R. Nunley, President, Montgomery College

Catherine B. Reynolds, Chairman and CEO, Catherine B. Reynolds Foundation, EduCap, Inc.

Arthur J. Rothkopf, Senior Vice President and Counselor to the President, US Chamber of Commerce; President Emeritus, Lafayette College

Richard (Rick) Stephens, Senior Vice President, Human Resources and Administration, the Boeing Company

Louis W. Sullivan, President Emeritus, Morehouse School of Medicine; former Secretary of the US Department of Health and Human Services

Sara Martinez Tucker, President and CEO, Hispanic Scholarship Fund

Richard Vedder, Adjunct Scholar, American Enterprise Institute, Distinguished Professor of Economics, Ohio University

Charles M. Vest, President Emeritus, Professor of Mechanical Engineering, Massachusetts Institute of Technology

David Ward, President of the American Council on Education (did not sign the final report)

Robert M. Zemsky, Chair and Professor, the Learning Alliance for Higher Education, University of Pennsylvania

Source: https://en.wikipedia.org/wiki/Commission_on_the_Future_of_Higher_Education.

NOTES

INTRODUCTION

1. Isocrates, *Isocrates II*, 179–366. Isocrates argues that by teaching his students rhetoric, he has taught them how to be better citizens and leaders of Athens. His work as an educator is worth more than any monetary donation he can give to Athens, since his teaching has provided for civic-minded and educated citizens who contribute to the orderly running of the city-state.

2. Though the "crisis" in higher education seems new, others have observed that this rhetoric of crisis is central to the modern humanities. For an in-depth study of the rhetoric of crisis in the modern university, see Reitter and Wellmon's *Permanent Crisis*.

3. Newfield, *Great Mistake*, 64.

4. For a discussion of the meaning of "public good" in economics, see the Wikipedia entry https://en.wikipedia.org/wiki/Public_good_(economics). For a discussion of "club goods" as distinguished from public goods, see https://en.wikipedia.org/wiki/Club_good.

5. Classifying higher education has often been difficult for economists and policymakers, though, since higher education tends to share some features of a public good, but it also has private benefits and it is, in current practice, rivalrous in that most institutions do not have open admissions policies. Despite the fact that higher education in the United States is treated more like a private good or "club good" in terms of how it is funded, some theorists of higher education point out that that does not change the fact that having more people with access to higher education is fundamentally good for the public and, in this way, means that higher education is ultimately a type of public good. In *The Great Mistake* Christopher Newfield argues that higher education is a "dual good" (65) since it has both private and public benefits, but he ultimately argues that we need to fund higher education appropriately to reap its public benefits.

6. Labaree, *Perfect Mess*, 57. See also *Higher Learning, Greater Good* by McMahon, who argues there are nonmarket benefits for higher education, too, which should go beyond future student earnings and national productivity to include such things as health, longevity, quality of life, the democratic functioning of institutions, the deepening of democracy and human rights, lower crime rates and corruption, social capital and mobility, and happiness. For more on the public benefits of higher education as a whole, see Owen-Smith's *Research Universities for the Public Good*.

7. For an estimate of current student loan debt outstanding, see "Student Loan Debt Clock," accessed October 11, 2021, https://finaid.org/loans/studentloandebtclock/.

8. See Gagliardi et al., *American College Presidents Study 2017*. The study by the American Council on Higher Education found that college presidents reported the communications issues that they felt least prepared to handle included fundraising, crisis management, and government relations. What is notable about these issues is that they are essentially external-facing and public in focus, perhaps with the exception of crisis management in some contexts.

9. Labaree, *Perfect Mess*, 181. According to Labaree, there are five defining characteristics of higher education: (1) institutional autonomy; (2) sensitivity to consumers; (3) broad array of constituencies; (4) ambiguity; (5) organizational complexity.

10. Collini, "Defending Universities."

11. "About," Postsecondary Value Commission, April 25, 2019, https://www.postsecondaryvalue.org/about/.

12. AAC&U, *How College Contributes*, quoted in "Is College Worth It? New BPC and AAC&U Research Brief on Public and Employer Perceptions," Bipartisan Policy Center, September 13, 2021, https://bipartisanpolicy.org/press-release/is-college-worth-it-new-bpc-and-aacu-research-brief-on-public-and-employer-perceptions/.

13. Bipartisan Policy Center and AAC&U, "Is College Worth the Time and Money?," 3–4.

14. Karen Tracy and Robert Asen have both made compelling cases for doing fieldwork of K–12 school boards to understand their deliberative significance. See Tracy, *Challenges of Ordinary Democracy*. See also Asen, *Democracy, Deliberation, and Education*.

15. For an explanation of the many missions and stakeholders of higher education, see Labaree, *Perfect Mess*. For a defense of how this multiplicity of missions and stakeholders is a strength of the US university, rather than a limitation, see Owen-Smith, *Research Universities for the Public Good*.

16. Asen, "Reflections," 124.

17. Camp, "Books or Bombs." Camp is the director of government relations at Teachers College, Columbia University, and draws from his experience in higher education lobbying to argue that institutions of higher education must do more to advocate for better public funding for higher education.

18. For Asen, see *Democracy*, Hlavacik, *Assigning Blame*. Hlavacik argues that we reconsider the rhetorical tactic of blame for pursuing K–12 and other education reform.

19. A surprising finding from this study is the lack of a distinct "HBCU perspective" during the discussions about the future of US higher education and its implications for accreditation. For more about the apparent lack of research on HBCUs and accreditation, see Fester, Gasman, and Nguyen, "We Know Very Little." Despite the fact that there was not much about HBCUs on the official record during the Spellings case, there were four ways that those from HBCUs participated or were represented during the policy process: (1) *Commission representation*: There was one representative on the Spellings Commission from an HBCU, Louis Sullivan, MD, former president of the Morehouse School of Medicine. During the time of the Spellings Commission, Sullivan also served as chair of the President's Commission on Historically Black Colleges and Universities (2002–9) and the President's Commission on HIV/AIDS. In Sullivan's introductory remarks to the Commission, he emphasized the role of education in helping to improve global public health literacy. (2) *Presidential leadership*: At the first Commission summit with working groups in 2007, forty-nine college presidents were present, including the president of Grambling State University, which is a public HBCU in Louisiana. In addition to this HBCU leadership, John Moder of the Hispanic Association of Colleges and Universities was also at this summit. (3) *Student testimony*: Testimony from a student at Howard University was included at the Commission's first summit, as well as student testimony from a student at St. Phillips Community College (a HBCU and Hispanic-serving institution) at the Nashville summit. Their remarks focused on issues of education affordability. (4) *Professional organizations*: The National Association of State Universities and Land-Grant Colleges (NASULGC) also provided remarks on the Spellings Commission. This professional organization's membership includes eighteen HBCUs and thirty-three tribal colleges. While some HBCU leaders and students were included in the policy process in the ways outlined above, it is notable that there was

no discussion on public record of how these education policies would impact HBCUs directly, even though the Commission's work would go on to influence accreditation standards. As one reviewer pointed out to me, there may be a rhetorical strategy at play here or possibly the suppression of the HBCU perspective.

20. For a robust reception study of the Spellings Commission, see Ruben et al., *Assessing the Impact*. Ruben's team at Rutgers was hired by the National Association of College and University Business Officers (NACUBO) to conduct a reception study of the Spellings Commission and its effects on higher education. For an analysis of the significance of the Spellings Commission's rhetoric in terms of organizational communication, see Lewis, *Organizational Change*. There have also been numerous articles written about the rhetoric of the Spellings Commission report, but to my knowledge there have no rhetorical studies of the argument strategies used by advocates in higher education *to respond* to the Spellings Commission, which is the primary focus of this inquiry.

21. For discussion of the new era of accountability in higher education policy, see chapter 2. Of course, calls for more information about higher education—and more accountability for colleges and universities—are not new. But prior to the Spellings Commission, "accountability" in higher education was largely governed by state regulatory agencies, private accrediting agencies, and a minimum cohort-default rate to maintain eligibility for federal student loans and grants. By contrast, one of the main concerns for the Spellings Commission was that universities were not doing enough to measure student-learning outcomes. Such a perception was supported by lower than usual completion rates among postsecondary students in the early 2000s and a perceived lack of pricing transparency about the cost of a college degree.

22. In particular, this book includes representative examples from the following: (1) academic news media, including the *Chronicle of Higher Education* and *Inside Higher Ed*, which provided extensive coverage of the Spellings Commission's work and also published numerous opinion pieces about it from many in higher education; (2) scholarly journals, which provided analyses of the significance of the Commission's work for many in higher education, such as the *Journal of Higher Education*, *Higher Education Quarterly*, *Higher Education Management and Policy*, and *Higher Education in Review*; (3) public responses to the Commission made by academic professional organizations such as the Association of American Universities (AAU) and the American Association of University Professors (AAUP) and professional organizations like the Modern Language Association (MLA) and the American Historical Association (AHA); (4) transcripts of government-sponsored forums, such as the U.S. Department of Education roundtables and hearings on the Spellings Report and congressional hearing transcripts from the reauthorization of the Higher Education Act from 2007 to 2009; and (5) graduation speeches and faculty meeting minute transcripts from public forums in higher education where the Spellings Commission was invoked or discussed.

23. Butler, "Ordinary, Incredulous," 17. The introduction to this volume was prefaced with concerns about the long-term impact of the Spellings Commission on higher education, specifically with metrics of accountability.

24. Williams, "Post-Welfare State University." Williams identifies five types of commentary about the university: (1) criticisms of academic capitalism; (2) criticisms of academic labor; (3) theoretical critiques of the university; (4) apologies or defenses; and (5) histories.

25. For "critical university studies," see Williams, "Deconstructing Academe." Defenses of the liberal arts and humanities have become a new genre of higher education writing all its own. For example, see Nussbaum, *Not for Profit*; Roth, *Beyond the University*; Zakaria, *In Defense of a Liberal Education*. Such defenses tend to fall into the category of either "apologies" (defenses) or "theoretical critiques" that Williams

identifies (see "Post-Welfare State University" and note 24). A classic example is a book like Bloom's *Closing of the American Mind*. However, unlike most of the older critiques, these newer ones have a more positive, manifesto-like tone that is future-facing. It is also worth noting that the issue of higher education's public funding crisis is increasingly *not* limited to the liberal arts and humanities. For example, educators in STEM fields have begun sounding alarm bells about the consequences of decreased public funding for research and how they are affected by funding cuts as well, which includes lack of access to the liberal arts and humanities for STEM students. For an account that refutes the typical humanities "crisis" narrative and instead focuses on issues of deprofessionalization and academic freedom, see Bérubé and Ruth, *Humanities, Higher Education, and Academic Freedom*.

26. Goldrick-Rab's research on how students finance their education and navigate the difficulties within the financial aid system has had a major impact on college campuses, including addressing food insecurity and aid. See Goldrick-Rab, *Paying the Price*.

27. For a new type of higher education history that focuses on its promise of a common good, see Dorn, *For the Common Good*. For an account of how austerity politics have shaped US higher education, see Fabricant and Brier, *Austerity Blues*.

28. Critiques of these kinds of handbooks often parallel a critique found in studies of ancient Greek rhetoric of what is known as "the handbook tradition" of rhetoric. For example, Athenian citizens had to respond to a rapidly changing political situation, since a democracy required more people to learn techniques of rhetoric to participate in the assembly and to defend themselves in the law courts or to press lawsuits. Rhetorical handbooks were primers on common types of arguments and ways of styling speech to help citizens participate in democracy. Rhetoric handbooks were often derided by educators and philosophers at that time, who argued that they were devoid of moral and ethical grounding or a more general theory about the subject.

29. Ruben and De Lisi, *Guide for Leaders in Higher Education*, 69.

30. Ibid., 80.

31. See Clifton, "Casting Public Imagination." Clifton argues that a decline in the English major is a crisis not of marketing but rather of public imagination. To overcome it, she encourages the productive orientation toward public life as central to the pedagogical work of English studies in higher education.

32. Medvetz, *Think Tanks in America*, 21, quoted in Staley, *Alternative Universities*, 69. See also Staley, *Alternative Universities*, 69–70. What I am defining here has a likeness to Staley's "humanist as policy expert," but one informed by the practices of rhetoric.

33. For the more basic recommendation that higher education advocates just need to "tell a better story," see Ruben et al., *Assessing the Impact*, 141.

34. For *topoi*, translated as "common topics" or "lines of argument" in classical rhetorical theory, see Aristotle's *Rhetoric* 1.2. For the revitalization of the *topoi* (or *loci communes*) in modern Western rhetorical theory, see Perelman and Olbrechts-Tyteca, *New Rhetoric*, 83–84. Because Aristotle does not define the *topoi* precisely, and in some cases he offers conflicting definitions, there have been many modern and contemporary attempts to reinterpret them. Rhetorical scholars agree that the topics are key to classical theories of invention. In reference to the significance of *New Rhetoric*'s rehabilitation of the *topoi*, see Crosswhite, *Deep Rhetoric*. Crosswhite has argued that the topoi and "technique of argumentation" in *New Rhetoric* is "not just a profound reinterpretation of rhetorical logos, it is also both an example of and an argument for the rhetorical virtue of copiousness. Since no single argument yields compelling truth (because choice and commitment always play a role), there is a need to develop as many arguments as possible from as many perspectives as possible in order to measure their relative strength,

in order to examine all the possible choices and commitments involved, and to consider where they may lead" (298). For more about the history of invention, see Lauer, *Invention in Rhetoric and Composition*. For an inquiry into what the classical concept of *topoi* can offer contemporary rhetorical theory, see Muckelbauer, *Future of Invention*. Kelly Pender emphasizes the *topoi* as productive of rhetoric in *Being at Genetic Risk*. This productive sense of *topoi* is also found in pedagogical work that focuses on how the topoi can be used to teach students how to create argument. For work on how *topoi* can be used in in academic contexts for teaching writing, see Wolfe, Olson, and Wilder, "Knowing What We Know."

35. Muller, *Tyranny of Metrics*, 18. Muller defines "metric fixation" as the "persistence of [the following] beliefs despite their unintended negative consequences when put into practice": "the belief that it is possible and desirable to replace judgment, acquired by personal experience and talent with numerical indicators of comparative performance based open standardization (metrics); the belief that making such metrics public (transparent) assures that institutions are actually carrying out their purposes (accountability); [and] the belief that the best way to motivate people within these organizations is by attaching rewards and penalties to their measured performance, rewards that are either monetary (pay-for-performance) or reputational (rankings)."

CHAPTER 1

1. Spellings, "National Dialogue."
2. The National Defense Education Act (NDEA) was passed in 1958 in response to Soviet dominance of the space race with the launch of the satellite Sputnik. The NDEA provided federal funding to "insure trained manpower of sufficient quality and quantity to meet the national defense needs of the United States." It authorized federal loans for college students for the first time, and it bolstered higher education with $1 billion (about $10 billion in 2022 dollars) in the areas of science, mathematics, and modern foreign languages while eliminating things such as college-level Latin except at the graduate level. The House report that recommended passage of the NDEA stated: "It is no exaggeration to say that America's progress in many fields of endeavor in the years ahead—in fact, the very survival of our free country—may depend in large part upon the education we provide for our young people now."
3. Spellings, "National Dialogue."
4. Kuehl, "Rhetorical Presidency."
5. U.S. Department of Higher Education, *Test of Leadership*, 21. https://files.eric.ed.gov/fulltext/ED493504.pdf.
6. Spellings, "National Dialogue."
7. Field, "Texas Millionaire."
8. Ibid.
9. Reported in Ruben et al., *Assessing the Impact*, 141.
10. Zemsky, "Rise and Fall."
11. Ibid.
12. Ruben et al., *Assessing the Impact*, 108.
13. U.S. Department of Higher Education, *Test of Leadership*, xii.
14. For an in-depth account of how the rhetorical trope of blame has been used to shape US education policy, see Hlavacik, *Assigning Blame*, 14.
15. Ruben et al., *Assessing the Impact*, 70.
16. Ibid.
17. Chambliss, "Flawed Metaphor."

18. Huot, "Consistently Inconsistent."

19. For an explication of the form/content dissociation, see Perelman and Olbrechts-Tyteca, *New Rhetoric*, 421.

20. Style is traditionally understood as one of the five canons of ancient Greek and Roman rhetoric, along with invention, arrangement, memory, and delivery. However, style in contemporary rhetorical theory is generally thought to encompass much *more* than the formal features of language and refer to whole systems of social practices. For example, see Hariman, *Political Style*. Hariman defines political style as "(1) a set of rules for speech and conduct guiding the alignment of signs and situations, or texts and acts, or behavior and place; (2) informing practices of communication and display; (3) operating through a repertoire of rhetorical conventions depending on aesthetic reactions; and (4) determining individual identity, providing social cohesion, and distributing power" (187). For a historical account of the concept of rhetorical style in the field of rhetoric and composition, see Butler, *Out of Style*.

21. Ruben et al., *Assessing the Impact*, 10.

22. For a definition of the term "political style" as I mean it here, see note 20.

23. Muller, *Tyranny of Metrics*, 18–19.

24. Hariman, *Political Style*, chap. 2.

25. Ultimately, there are three reasons I want to focus on what I am calling managerial style when analyzing contemporary policy cases in higher education advocacy contexts such as the Spellings case. First, since the 1990s, when Hariman advanced his thesis about realist style, there have been movements in higher education away from purely market-based systems that were being put into place strictly for efficiency, to today's contractual mechanisms and performance measurement through audit and review, which were advocated for in the Spellings Report and beyond. Second, the political world of "sheer power, constant calculation, and emotional control" identified with the realist style appears to have given way in the twenty-first century to a redefinition of the citizen-consumer's place in it. For example, not only do consumers have a choice in regard to where and how they receive their services, but it is now expected that they should be actively involved as stakeholders in determining what services should be provided by higher education as well. Margaret Spellings's call for ways she might navigate her daughter's college experience in terms of cost-versus-value using a bluebook for higher education is emblematic of this change. What is new here is recognition of the technologies of self that individuals employ to implicate themselves in their own management. Third, and finally, managerial style in higher education policy contexts highlights the way public services like higher education are increasingly less like the production of sheer power and instead produce their own governance structures. The style of policy discourse public higher education has adopted is more crucial for its success than in the past, as can be seen in the failure of the Spellings case versus the successes of previous presidential commissions on higher education.

26. See, in general, Berg and Seeber, *Slow Professor*; Coleman and Kamboureli, *Retooling the Humanities*. In making their case for the "slow professor" by challenging the culture of speed in learning, teaching, and researching in higher education settings, Berg and Seeber build on Coleman and Kamboureli's research, who argue for "time as an infrastructural need in the humanities" (55).

27. See Butler, *Out of Style*, 144. As Butler points out, to suggest otherwise about the nature of styles of discourse is to deny the way in which "form and content are inexorably linked."

28. See Vivian, "Style, Rhetoric, and Postmodern Culture." The need for us to focus on aesthetics is also emphasized in Vivian's critique of Hariman's work. Vivian contends that the issue of style has not been given rightful attention in the field of rhetoric. He

argues: "One might propose that the meaning of rhetoric as such matters less than the social practices it enables" (26).

29. In Hariman's *Political Style*, he outlines four stylistic types that are helpful starting points when considering policymaking language in higher education contexts: (1) the realist style (exemplified by Machiavelli's *The Prince*); (2) the republican style (exemplified by Cicero's *Letters*); (3) the bureaucratic style (exemplified by Kafka's *The Castle*); and (4) the courtly style (exemplified by Ryszard Kapuściński's *The Emperor*). For Hariman, the realist style creates a world of sheer power, constant calculation, and emotional control; this style, he argued, is the common sense of modern political science. In contrast, the courtly style is characterized by high decorousness, hierarchies, and fixation on the body of the sovereign; for example, this style infuses mass media coverage of the American presidency. The republican style, on the other hand, promotes the art of oratory, consensus, and civility; it informs our ideal of deliberative, democratic conversation. And finally, the bureaucratic style emphasizes institutional procedures, official character, and the priority of written communication; this style structures our everyday life.

30. Hariman, *Political Style*, 53.

31. Ibid., chap. 4. In contrast to the realist style, Hariman argues that the republican style is embodied in the Roman orator Marcus Tullius Cicero, who was a Roman statesman, lawyer, scholar, and philosopher at the time great political crises resulted in the Roman Empire. Contra Miller, Cicero would have argued that "it is not by muscle, speed, or physical dexterity that great things are achieved, but by reflection, force of character, and judgment." Cicero, *De Senectute*, sec. 17.

32. Hariman, *Political Style*, 193. See also Markovits, *Politics of Sincerity*. Markovits argues that the search for "straight talk" or sincerity in the public arena can constitute a dangerous distraction from factual truth and the ethical import and real-world consequences of political statements.

33. Ruben et al., *Assessing the Impact*, 10.

34. Hariman, *Political Style*, 4.

35. See Fitzsimons, "Managerialism and Education."

36. See Sullivan, "Closer Look at Education."

37. Asen, "Reflections on the Role of Rhetoric," 126.

38. U.S. Department of Higher Education, "Test of Leadership," 27.

39. Asen, *Invoking the Invisible Hand*, 14.

40. Perelman and Olbrechts-Tyteca, *New Rhetoric*, iv. The persuasive appeal to realist rhetoric in everyday argumentation has long been recognized in rhetorical theory. Perelman and Olbrechts-Tyteca devote an entire chapter to elucidate that technique of argumentation that springs from realist/idealist tendency to dissociate "the real" from "the apparent" in philosophical arguments: "While appearances can be opposed to each other," they point out, "reality is [true] coherent" (416).

41. See Markwardt, "From Sputnik to the Spellings Commission." Markwardt observes that the Spellings Commission was significant in the history of higher education policy because it focused on the market to the exclusion of other issues; it also represented a shift from higher education as a form of national defense to higher education as key to marketplace competition.

42. U.S. Department of Higher Education, "Test of Leadership," xii.

43. For the "strict father model of morality" in American politics, see Lakoff, "Metaphor, Morality, and Politics"; Lakoff, *Moral Politics*, 29–30; Lakoff and Johnson, "Conceptual Metaphor in Everyday Language," 453.

44. U.S. Department of Higher Education, "Test of Leadership," xii.

45. Hariman, *Political Style*, 44.

46. U.S. Department of Higher Education, "Test of Leadership," xii.

47. Hariman, *Political Style*, 44.
48. U.S. Department of Higher Education, "Test of Leadership," xi.
49. Hariman, *Political Style*, 48.
50. U.S. Department of Higher Education, "Test of Leadership," 21.
51. Harvey, *Brief History of Neoliberalism*, 3.
52. McKenna and Graham, "Technocratic Discourse," 224. Technocratic discourse is a hybrid discourse that draws interdiscursively from scientific discourse and from technological discourse. It also draws from the historical lexico-grammars of managerialism, the military, and religion, in particular the scholastics. The linguistic markers of technocratic discourse include (a) heavy reliance on nominalizations; (b) abstract words and processes; and (c) limited use of verbs, which contributes to an overall lack of human agency.
53. Harvey, *Brief History of Neoliberalism*, 66.
54. Muller, *Tyranny of Metrics*, chap. 15. Muller describes eleven unintended but negative consequences of relying exclusively on standardized metrics for accountability: (1) goal displacement through diversion of effort to what gets measured; (2) romoting short-termism; (3) costs in employee time; (4) diminishing utility; (5) rule cascade; (6) rewarding luck; (7) discouraging risk-taking; (8) discouraging innovation; (9) discouraging cooperation and common purpose; (10) degradation of work; (11) cost to productivity.
55. U.S. Department of Higher Education, "Test of Leadership," 21.
56. Miller, "Opportunity, Opportunism, and Progress," 89.
57. Ibid., 85.
58. Dunmire, *Projecting the Future Through Political Discourse*, 62.
59. U.S. Department of Higher Education, "Test of Leadership," 29.
60. Fairclough, "Language and Neo-Liberalism," 147–48.
61. U.S. Department of Higher Education, "Test of Leadership," xii.
62. Ibid., 25.
63. Roberts, "No One Is Perfect"; see also Styhre, *Management and Neoliberalism*.
64. U.S. Department of Higher Education, "Test of Leadership," 16.
65. Chaput, "Rhetorical Circulation in Late Capitalism," 2. As Chaput argues, the "neoliberal landscape consists of blurred boundaries that fold into one another: information flows almost instantaneously, commodities and people transgress national boundaries, time accelerates, space collapses, and distinctions between such classic demarcations as agent and subject or politics and economics erode."
66. Chambliss, "Flawed Metaphor."
67. See Huot, "Consistently Inconsistent," 504.
68. Ibid., 519.
69. See Chambliss, "Flawed Metaphor."
70. Ruben et al., *Assessing the Impact*, 75. Ruben et al. identify the following "traditional core values of the academic culture": freedom of expression; collegial decision-making; creating, advancing, and impacting knowledge; primary loyalty to discipline rather than institutions; higher education as unique and special—not a business; students are learners, not customers; self-determination (individual and institutional); the faculty *as* the university, particularly in terms of input and influence; customization of processes and procedures; aversion to board, state, accrediting, and Department of Education perspectives as important in decision-making.
71. The concept of *stasis* comes from ancient Greek and means a "stopping" or "standing still." Typically, a stasis is a type of question that names a common point of public argument about a public issue. The five *stases* in policy debate include fact (does an issue exist?), definition (how do we define the issue?), quality (how bad is the issue?),

and policy (what should we do about the issue?). As Hlavacik observes of the debate about *Nation at Risk*, using self-blame allowed the public debate to move beyond the first stage of fact to the other *stases* of definition, quality, and policy. "This is a subtle, but valuable strategic advantage of self-blaming," Hlavacik observes, "and *Nation at Risk* hit it out of the park" (52). For more on how the stases can help identify disciplinary differences in argument style, see Fahnestock and Secor, "Stases in Scientific and Literary Argument." For a contemporary study of how the stases can help illuminate fundamental disagreements about textual interpretation of laws and policies, see Camper, *Arguing over Texts*.

72. See Gounari, "Contesting the Cynicism of Neoliberal Discourse."

73. For how multiple reports extend the bounds of a rhetorical situation, see Rude, "Toward an Expanded Concept of Rhetorical Delivery." As Rude's work would indicate, it is common for reports like the Spellings Report to be a first step in a much longer effort to institute social action and policy change.

74. For the College Transparency Act, see https://www.congress.gov/bill/117th-congress/senate-bill/839/text?r=2&s=1.

75. The American Council on Education (ACE) 2023 Report on American College Presidents Survey (ACPS) found that only slightly more than half of presidents "arrived to the presidency through the traditional faculty or academic pathway" (1). The report showed an increase in presidents who approached the presidency "through alternatives outside the traditional pathway," including the public, nonprofit, and business sectors (1). American Council on Education (ACE), *2023 Report on American College Presidents Survey (ACPS)*.

76. I use the term "reciprocity" here to emphasize the need for those in higher education and policymakers to recognize how we are bound by a *shared* public life.

CHAPTER 2

1. For example, in K–12 contexts, see Asen, *Democracy, Deliberation, and Education*; Asen, *School Choice and the Betrayal of Democracy*.

2. See Asen, "Lyndon Baines Johnson and George W. Bush on Education Reform."

3. Green, "Politics of Literacy," 370. Green explains how the rhetoric of accountability has become a bipartisan political issue that is increasingly difficult for educators to challenge.

4. The issue of "accountability" in public arguments about the Spellings Report can be said to fan out into five argumentative *topoi*. For "fan-type" arguments, see Perelman and Olbrechts-Tyteca, *New Rhetoric*, 431; Camper, *Arguing over Texts*, 72–74; Anderson, "Exploring the Multimodal Gutter."

5. U.S. Department of Higher Education, "Test of Leadership," 20–21.

6. For the claim that the accountability database was the most controversial recommendation of the Spellings Report, see Huot, "Consistently Inconsistent," 519.

7. See Ward, "Current Concerns and Future Prospects."

8. Quoted in Ruben et al., *Assessing the Impact*, 103.

9. "Standardized self-evaluations" are also considered a standard practice under New Public Management (NPM). See Lorenz, "If You're So Smart," 37.

10. Ohmann, "Historical Reflections on Accountability," 24.

11. Ibid., 28.

12. Asen, "Lyndon Baines Johnson and George W. Bush."

13. U.S. Department of Education, "Nation at Risk."

14. McIntush, "Defining Education."

15. Asen, "Lyndon Baines Johnson and George W. Bush," 303.

16. Kuehl, "Rhetorical Presidency," 347.
17. Ibid., 307.
18. Ewell, "Assessment and Accountability."
19. For the "external improvement paradigm" in relation to testing in general, see Phillips, *Testing Controversy*.
20. Kuh, "Risky Business," 32.
21. Much discussed by Perelman and Olbrechts-Tyteca in *New Rhetoric*, the paradigm example of dissociation is the appearance/reality pair often found in philosophical argumentation. Using the perennial case of a stick submerged in water, they explain that the stick *appears* (term 1) as though it is bent when in *reality* (term 2) it is not. The example of the bent stick illustrates how a dissociation, which functions by breaking apart the seemingly unified concept of being into the appearance/reality pair, "brings about a more or less profound change in the conceptual data that are used as the basis of [a future] argument" (412).
22. Ibid.
23. Ibid., 424.
24. Ritivoi, "Dissociation of Concepts in Context," 185.
25. Ibid.
26. Frank, "Dialectical Rapprochement in the New Rhetoric," 123.
27. In general, see Schiappa, *Defining Reality*.
28. Perelman and Olbrechts-Tyteca, *New Rhetoric*, 420.
29. Ibid., 83.
30. Camper, *Arguing over Texts*, 72–74. As Camper points out, these "fan-type" dissociations emerge when advocates are "faced with some interpretive difficulty or exigence," which can be resolved only through additional dissociations. Each dissociation fans out from an assumed fundamental dissociation of the term "accountability" into market accountability/educational accountability.
31. Bennett, "Underinvesting in the Future."
32. Tilghman, "2007 President's Commencement Remarks."
33. See Kimball, *Orators and Philosophers*. Kimball argues that we can understand the history of liberal education as an interplay of two distinct traditions: one grounded in the oratorical tradition (*artes liberales*) and one in the philosophic tradition (liberal-free). The liberal-free tradition is born of the Enlightenment but is a revival of philosophic tradition and fascination with Socratic critique and mathematical laws. It is characterized by the following: freedom, intellect and rationality, critical skepticism, tolerance, egalitarianism, volition of the individual, and the Kantian notion that the search for truth is more important than attaining truth itself. By contrast, the *artes liberales* tradition is born of Renaissance humanism, and it is a revival of the oratorical tradition of the Romans with emphasis on the "good man speaking well."
34. For the function of epideictic rhetoric or "maintenance" discourse, see Perelman and Olbrechts-Tyteca, *New Rhetoric*, 51; Cloud, "Social Consequences of Dissociation," 163. Cloud points out that later work from Perelman and Olbrechts-Tyteca further emphasizes the necessity of maintaining public adherence to a position over time, a key function of *epideictic* rhetoric in a democratic society in which public attitudes evolve.
35. Ruben et al., *Assessing the Impact*, 146.
36. Travis Reindl, then state policy director and assistant to the president of the American Association of State Colleges and Universities, qtd. in Lederman, "Testing, Testing."
37. For the Annapolis Group of Liberal Arts Colleges, see https://www.annapolisgroup.org/. Despite its name, the Annapolis Group has more than one hundred liberal arts member colleges nationwide. Their shared mission states that "a liberal arts

education offers students the most valuable preparation for a lifetime of meaningful and productive work in an ever-changing world." For a list of participating colleges, see https://www.annapolisgroup.org/_files/ugd/88781c_e6b2ec097ef64ec8807971f00b2d59b0.pdf.

38. Nelson, "Remarks for Ivory Tower Overhaul."
39. Tilghman, "2007 President's Commencement Remarks."
40. Nelson, "Remarks for Ivory Tower Overhaul."
41. Graff and Birkenstein, "Progressive Case for Educational Standardization," 16–18.
42. Ibid., 17.
43. Ibid., 18.
44. Maher, "Divided by Loyalty."
45. In contrast to Nelson and Tilghman's arguments, which focused on freedom of the individual (in the liberal-free, philosophical tradition), Graff and Birkenstein's argument focuses on a shared culture (and is more akin to the *artes liberales*, "oratorical" tradition of the liberal arts). For an account of the history of these traditions, see Kimball, *Orators and Philosophers*.
46. Schiappa, *Defining Reality*, 39.
47. Nelson, "Remarks for Ivory Tower Overhaul."
48. Adler-Kassner and Harrington, "Reframing the Accountability Debate."
49. For a recent account of how K–12 teachers publicly advocate for their professional authority and expertise, see Garahan, "Public Work of Identity Performance."
50. Toth, "Regulating the New Consumerism."
51. Moen, "Aristotle in an Era of Accountability," 14.
52. Berdahl, "Comments on the Second Draft."
53. Nussbaum, *Not for Profit*.
54. Graff and Birkenstein, "Progressive Case for Educational Standardization."
55. Quoted in Lederman, "Testing, Testing."
56. Adler-Kassner and Harrington, "Reframing the Accountability Debate."
57. Graff and Birkenstein, "Progressive Case for Educational Standardization," 17.

CHAPTER 3

1. Fitzpatrick, *Generous Thinking*, 193.
2. Newfield, *Great Mistake*, 76.
3. Winslow, "Undeserving Professor," 228.
4. Clifton, "Casting Public Imagination for the Evolving Major."
5. See Heifetz, Grashow, and Linsky, *Practice of Adaptive Leadership*.
6. Political theorist Iris Marion Young distinguishes the goals of the deliberative democrat from the activist. See Young, "Activist Challenges to Deliberative Democracy," 687.
7. Labaree, *Perfect Mess*, 196.
8. Williams, "Post-Welfare State University."
9. See Labaree, *Perfect Mess*. Labaree argues that "college is a private good to the extent that its benefits accrue primarily to the individuals who receive the education and the resulting diploma. College is a public good to the extent that its benefits go to the population as a whole, including both people who do and do not attend college" (87).
10. Newfield, *Great Mistake*, 64. In contrast to Newfield, Labaree argues that what we are experiencing is not a fall from a golden age, but a "regression to the mean." Based on this logic, higher education is understood as a "distinctively private good"

(not a public good). According to Labaree, at least, in the mid-twentieth century "Americans went through an intense but brief infatuation with higher education as a public good." Other than that time, Labaree believes it has been a distinctively private good. He also thinks it follows that "one conclusion is that the golden age of the American University in the mid-twentieth century was a one-off event. Wars may be endemic, but the Cold War was unique. So American university administrators and professors need to stop pining for a return to the good old days and learn how to live in the post–Cold War era" (*Perfect Mess*, 156).

11. Schiappa, *Defining Reality*, 40–41.

12. How we choose to define something as essentially public or private in turn structures the conditions under which people feel a responsibility to do something about the problem(s). For the importance of the public/private distinction in this regard, see Fraser, "Rethinking the Public Sphere."

13. For "framing," see Fischer, *Reframing Public Policy*; Hull, "Political Limits of the Rights Frame." My use of the term "framing" in this context is derived from work on "master frames" in policy cases and social movements by Fischer, Hull, and others. By "frame," I refer to how some discursive constructions provide a dominant lens through which policy is interpreted.

14. Perelman and Olbrechts-Tyteca, *New Rhetoric*.

15. For "value hierarchies" as I mean them here, see Perelman and Olbrechts-Tyteca, *New Rhetoric*, 80–81.

16. AAC&U, "Statement on Spellings Commission Report."

17. Breneman, "Comments on the Spellings Commission Report."

18. Though these examples frequently invoke the rhetoric of citizenship for higher education, I use "public" instead of "civic" to describe this strategy because it more broadly captures the way that arguers seek to strengthen the public sphere. This terminology also avoids the legal connotations of citizenship which excludes undocumented and international students and scholars who make up a large and important part of US higher education. For a critique of educators' "rote invocation of citizenship" to justify literacy practices in the writing classroom, see Wan, "In the Name of Citizenship." For a critique of how a rhetoric of citizenship has shaped disciplinary histories of rhetoric, see Chávez, "Beyond Inclusion."

19. The MLA was started in 1883 and is now the largest professional organization uniting faculty in the humanities in North America. It played a major role in shaping faculty perceptions of the Spellings Commission. In addition to a formal response from the executive board and the response from president Gerald Graff, the annual conference hosted discussions about the Spellings Commission for the wider membership. The AAUP was founded in 1915 and is the primary professional organization that unites all faculty member in US higher education. For an in-depth history of the founding of the organization, see Tiede, *University Reform*.

20. Ibid.

21. See Kimball, *Orators and Philosophers*. The liberal-free tradition is born of the Enlightenment but is a revival of philosophic tradition and fascination with Socratic critique and mathematical laws. It is characterized by thefreedom, intellect and rationality, critical skepticism, tolerance, egalitarianism, volition of the individual, and the Kantian notion that the search for truth is more important than attaining truth itself.

22. Nelson, "Remarks for Ivory Tower Overhaul."

23. See Brann, *Paradoxes of Education in a Republic*. Brann argues that higher education should not be practical, but instead "prepractical," since it should emphasize those foundational theories, principles, and ends that prepare one for the practical aspects of life. Brann's inquiry into the paradoxes of education brings clarity to Nelson's

reprioritization of guiding values for higher education, whereby "good citizenship" is the not the goal, but a byproduct of a good education.

24. Ibid.

25. For the "liberal-free tradition" in the history of liberal arts curriculum, see Kimball, *Orators and Philosophers*, and note 21.

26. Nelson, "Remarks for Ivory Tower Overhaul."

27. Graff and Birkenstein, "Progressive Case for Educational Standardization," 16–18.

28. Ibid., 17.

29. Ibid., 18.

30. AAUP, "Statement of the Committee on Government Relations."

31. Ibid.

32. Ibid.

33. Nussbaum, *Not for Profit*.

34. For example, see Nussbaum, Commencement Address; "Founders Day Speaker [Martha C. Nussbaum] Celebrates the Liberal Arts"; Lawrence University News, "Martha C. Nussbaum: Liberal Education."

35. Nussbaum, Commencement Address.

36. Ibid.

37. For a definition of "social knowledge" as I mean it in this context, see Farrell, "Knowledge, Consensus, and Rhetorical Theory"; Farrell, "Social Knowledge II."

38. See Roberts-Miller, *Deliberate Conflict*.

39. Roberts-Miller originally defines six different models of the public sphere. I focus only on the five that I found more commonly in this case.

40. Maher, "Divided by Loyalty," 319.

41. Ibid., 37. According to Roberts-Miller, "Communitarians argue that the distinction [between the liberal and interest-based] is essentially false—the liberal model necessarily ends up in the interest-based model due to its unwillingness to impose a particular set of morals on its citizens."

42. See Cottom, *Lower Ed*. Cottom defines "lower ed" as being more expansive than just for-profit colleges: "Lower Ed refers to credential expansion created by structural changes in how we work, unequal group access to favorable higher education schemes, and the risk shift of job training, from states and companies to individuals and families, exclusively for profit.... Lower Ed is, first and foremost, a set of institutions organized to commodify social inequalities ... and make no social contributions beyond the assumed indirect effect of greater individual human capital. But Lower Ed is not just a collection of schools or set of institutional practices like profit taking and credential granting. Lower Ed encompasses all credential expansion that leverage our faith in education without challenging its market imperatives and that preserves the status quo of race, class, and gender inequalities in education and work. When we offer more credentials in lieu of a stronger social contract, it is Lower Ed. When we ask for social insurance and get workforce training, it is Lower Ed. When we ask for justice and get 'opportunity,' it is Lower Ed" (12).

43. Ibid., 186.

44. Ibid., 672.

45. Young, "Activist Challenges to Deliberative Democracy," 686.

46. Muller, *Tyranny of Metrics*, 40.

47. Perelman and Olbrechts-Tyteca, *New Rhetoric*, 51.

48. National Task Force on Civic Learning and Democratic Engagement and Association of American Colleges and Universities, *Crucible Moment*.

49. Butler, "Ordinary, Incredulous," 17.

CHAPTER 4

1. Alexander, "Remarks."
2. Staley, *Alternative Universities*, 69–70.
3. For representative examples, see Craig and Blue, *New U*; Czerniewicz, "Unbundling and Rebundling"; Boggs et al., "Abolitionist University Studies."
4. Kanelos, "We Can't Wait."
5. Ibid.
6. See Jameson, "Politics of Utopia." As Jameson points out, it is important to oppose political attacks on the idea of utopia, as these are usually reactionary statements on the behalf of the currently powerful. What I am taking issue with is those who want to build a utopia-for-the-few for students alongside a dystopia-for-the-many.
7. Staley, *Alternative Universities*, 12.
8. Owen-Smith, *Research Universities and the Public Good*.
9. Mitchell and King, *How to Run a College*, 140.
10. Ibid.
11. Davidson, *New Education*, 13.
12. See Berlant, *Cruel Optimism*. We need to avoid what Berlant calls "cruel optimism," which is thinking and saying that things will get better without doing the work of together imagining how.
13. Roberts-Miller, *Deliberate Conflict*, 184–85. Roberts-Miller cites work on deliberative democracy from political theorist James Fearon, who points out the "psychological consequences of continually making that argument [for the public good] might cause even a very cynical person to believe it." Drawing from the rhetorical theory of Perelman and Olbrechts-Tyteca, she also emphasizes that the public/private distinction is rhetorical, insofar as it "amounts to how one makes one's argument, the reasons one gives" (81). See also Fraser, "Rethinking the Public Sphere."
14. Heifetz, Grashow, and Linsky, *Practice of Adaptive Leadership*, who argue that the single greatest failure of leadership is incorrectly differentiating between technical problems and adaptive challenges.
15. Asen, *Democracy, Deliberation, and Education*,146.
16. Ibid., 174.
17. See Tracy, *Challenges of Ordinary Democracy*, 125–26. Following Tracy, the argument for prioritizing trust building in such contexts is consistent with other studies of public deliberation.
18. Berg and Seeber, *Slow Professor*, 55.
19. Allen, *Talking to Strangers*, 157.
20. Gavazzi and Gee, *Land-Grant Universities for the Future*, 30.
21. Ibid., 140. Andreea Ritivoi also uses Allen's concept of political friendship to argue for enlarging our sense of civic inclusiveness "unconstrained by an ethics of nationality." See Ritivoi, *Intimate Strangers*, 251.
22. Aristotle, *Aristotle's Metaphysics*, 1045a8–10: "In the case of all things which have several parts and in which the totality is not, as it were, a mere heap, but the whole is something besides [other than] the parts, there is a cause."
23. Asen, *Democracy, Deliberation, and Education*, 157.
24. Ibid.
25. Allen, *Talking to Strangers*, 153.
26. Aristotle, *Rhetoric* 1.2.1.
27. Roberts-Miller, *Deliberate Conflict*, 187.
28. Fitzpatrick, *Generous Thinking*, 231.
29. Ibid., 191.

30. Roberts-Miller, *Deliberate Conflict*, 166. See also Eberly, "From Writers, Audiences, and Communities to Publics."
31. Owen-Smith, *Research Universities and the Public Good*, 54.
32. "Community Think Tank." The website introduces students, teachers, and community members to the inner workings of the Think Tank model. As a model for deliberative dialogue and change, it suggests one way how—together—we could begin to more effectively respond to problems in higher education as public advocates.
33. See Dewey, "Quest for Certainty." A central focus of Dewey's pragmatism is his criticism of the tradition of ethical thought, and its tendency to seek solutions to problems in dogmatic principles and simplistic criteria that are incapable of dealing effectively with the changing requirements of human events. In brief, ideals and values must be deliberated about with respect to their social consequences.
34. For "rivaling," see Flower, Long, and Higgins, *Learning to Rival*. In this context, learning to "rival" means learning to actively seek out rival hypotheses and negotiate alternative perspectives as part of an intercultural inquiry.
35. Flower, "Intercultural Knowledge Building," 258.
36. For an explanation of higher education's stakeholder's, see Ruben and De Lisi, *Guide for Leaders*.
37. Critical incident interviewing is one among many strategies offered by Linda Flower to elicit situated knowledge. It is based on John C. Flanagan's work on the critical incident technique. For more on how to conduct critical incident interviews in community literacy studies, see Flower, *Community Literacy*, 28.
38. See "Community Think Tank."
39. See Long, *Responsive Rhetorical Art*.
40. See Flower, *Outcomes of Engaged Education*.
41. Clifton, "Casting Public Imagination for the Evolving Major."
42. Roberts-Miller, *Deliberate Conflict*, 197.

CHAPTER 5

1. For the College Scorecard, see https://collegescorecard.ed.gov. The website was substantially updated in February 2022. Prospective students and their parents or guardians can use the Scorecard to learn graduation rate and the earnings of former students, how much debt they can expect to take on, and compare schools based on graduates' earnings and how those earnings compare to workers without a degree. NPR's Cory Turner likens the updated Scorecard to "a shopping mall." See Turner, "Want to Find an Affordable College?"
2. Hillman and Weichman, "Education Deserts," 24.
3. Muller, *Tyranny of Metrics*, 176–77.
4. Ward, "Current Concerns and Future Prospects."
5. Winslow, "Undeserving Professor," 231.
6. See Daniels, Shreve, and Spector, *What Universities Owe Democracy*.
7. See the College Scorecard, note 1.
8. Turner, "President Obama's New 'College Scorecard.'" In a 2015 interview with Turner, sociologist Sara Goldrick-Rab stated that the College Scorecard was "technically good data to have" when it was released in 2015 but that it didn't actually help potential students to know what to do (also see above). President of Trinity Washington University Pat McGuire argued that the website consisted largely of "factoids" that reflect traditional, national norms that don't reflect who we [Trinity Washington University] are. McGuire's concern was that a school that serves vulnerable students can't be judged

by Scorecard metrics alone. For example, "Students often take eight, even ten years to graduate. They might go part time. They might leave and come back. The Scorecard doesn't capture that level of nuance," argued McGuire.

9. Turner, "President Obama's New 'College Scorecard.'"
10. Jaschik, "House Approves College Transparency Act."
11. IHEP, "IHEP Celebrates House Passage."
12. Alexander, "Accountability In Higher Education," 3.
13. Ibid.
14. Ibid.
15. Ibid.
16. Spellings, "Congress Digs a Moat."
17. Toth, "Regulating the New Consumerism."
18. On making economic rationality a reality in higher education in general, see Winslow, "Undeserving Professor." For the idea that there is a widespread sense that capitalism is the only political and economic system, see Fisher, *Capitalist Realism*. Fisher raises the idea of a "business ontology," in which social purposes and objectives are understood exclusively in business terms. Thus, ideas for improving education and healthcare are erroneously based on the assumption that the market best serves public needs.
19. The thirty-member Postsecondary Value Commission includes Margaret Spellings. For a list of Commission participants, see "Meet the Commission," Postsecondary Value Commission, https://postsecondaryvalue.org/members/. The Commission's members, consisting of higher ed experts and national leaders, were brought together to "examine, explore, and define the value of postsecondary education in the U.S."
20. Gates Foundation, "Postsecondary Value Commission Report."
21. Postsecondary Value Commission, "Equitable Value," 14.
22. Labaree, *Perfect Mess*, 194.
23. I am not the first to observe the abundance of cautionary notes (or "tool tips") when using the Value Equity Explorer. For example, see Jaschik, "Gates Foundation Effort." Jaschik points out that another weakness of the tool is the major limitation in existing data about median earnings measures ten years after undergraduate enrollment by race or gender.
24. See Muller, *Tyranny of Metrics*, chap. 11.
25. Ibid., 4.
26. Butler, "Ordinary, Incredulous," 174. Butler calls for a reanimation of critique to deal with this problem. They argue that "we need to reanimate critique as precisely a way of thinking about the competing schemes of evaluation and evaluating them" (147). Part of the problem is that our current sense of evaluation and of metrics is limited to what can be quantified.
27. Ibid., 18.

EPILOGUE

1. Owen-Smith, *Research Universities and the Public Good*.
2. Goodnight, "Personal, Technical, and Public Spheres," 198.
3. See Montgomery and Whittaker, "Reimagining Academic Leadership."

BIBLIOGRAPHY

Adler-Kassner, Linda, and Susanmarie Harrington. "Reframing the Accountability Debate." *Inside Higher Ed*, April 23, 2009. https://www.insidehighered.com/views/2009/04/23/reframing-accountability-debate.
Alexander, Lamar. "Accountability In Higher Education." Presented at the U.S. Senate, Washington, DC, May 24, 2007. https://justfacts.votesmart.org/public-statement/262859/accountability-in-higher-education#.UlIzLWK-vog.
———. "Remarks of U.S. Senator Lamar Alexander." A National Dialogue: The Secretary of Education's Commission on the Future of Higher Education. Nashville, TN, December 9, 2005.
Allen, Danielle S. *Talking to Strangers: Anxieties of Citizenship Since Brown v. Board of Education*. Chicago: University of Chicago Press, 2006.
American Association of University Professors (AAUP). "Beyond Crude Measurement and Consumerism." September 9, 2010. https://www.aaup.org/article/beyond-crude-measurement-and-consumerism.
———. "Statement of the Committee on Government Relations Regarding the Report *A Test of Leadership: Charting the Future of U.S. Higher Education*." 2006. https://web.archive.org/web/20071013052745/http://www.aaup.org/AAUP/GR/federal/FutureofHigherEd/spellrep.htm?PF=1.
The American College President Study. "Summary Profile—American College President Study." Accessed October 11, 2021. https://www.aceacps.org/summary-profile/.
American Council on Education (ACE). *2023 Report on American College Presidents Survey (ACPS)*. 2023. https://www.acenet.edu/Documents/American-College-President-IX-2023.pdf.
Anderson, Amy. "Exploring the Multimodal Gutter: What Dissociation Can Teach Us About Multimodality." *Enculturation* 25 (October 17, 2017). https://www.enculturation.net/exploring_the_multimodal_gutter.
Annapolis Group. "About." Accessed April 11, 2022. https://www.annapolisgroup.org/about.
Aristotle. *Aristotle's Metaphysics*. Translated by Joe Sachs. Santa Fe, NM: Green Lion Press, 1999.
———. *On Rhetoric: A Theory of Civic Discourse*. Translated by George Alexander Kennedy. New York: Oxford University Press, 1991.
———. *Rhetoric*. Translated by Joe Sachs. Focus Philosophical Library. Newburyport, MA: Focus, 2009.
Asen, Robert. *Democracy, Deliberation, and Education*. University Park: Penn State University Press, 2015.
———. *Invoking the Invisible Hand: Social Security and the Privatization Debates*. Rhetoric and Public Affairs Series. East Lansing: Michigan State University Press, 2009.
———. "Lyndon Baines Johnson and George W. Bush on Education Reform: Ascribing Agency and Responsibility Through Key Policy Terms." *Rhetoric and Public Affairs* 15, no. 2 (2012): 289–317.

———. "Reflections on the Role of Rhetoric in Public Policy." *Rhetoric and Public Affairs* 13, no. 1 (2010): 121–43.

———. *School Choice and the Betrayal of Democracy: How Market-Based Education Reform Fails Our Communities.* University Park: Penn State University Press, 2021.

Association of American Colleges and Universities (AAC&U). *How College Contributes to Workforce Success: Employer Views.* 2021. https://dgmg81phhvh63.cloudfront.net/content/user-photos/Research/PDFs/AACUEmployerReport2021.pdf.

———. "Statement on Spellings Commission Report." September 26, 2006. https://news.sfsu.edu/aacu-statement-spellings-commission-report-president-corrigan.

Bennett, Douglas C. "Underinvesting in the Future." *Chronicle of Higher Education*, September 1, 2006. https://www.chronicle.com/article/underinvesting-in-the-future/.

Berdahl, Robert. "Comments on the Second Draft of the Report of the Commission on the Future of Higher Education." Association of American Universities, July 31, 2006. https://web.archive.org/web/20060811065202/http://www.aau.edu/education/AAU_Response_to_Higher_Education_Commission_Second_Draft_Report-2006-07-31.pdf.

Berg, Maggie, and Barbara Karolina Seeber. *The Slow Professor: Challenging the Culture of Speed in the Academy.* Toronto: University of Toronto Press, 2016.

Berlant, Lauren. *Cruel Optimism.* Durham: Duke University Press, 2011.

Bérubé, Michael, and Jennifer Ruth. *The Humanities, Higher Education, and Academic Freedom: Three Necessary Arguments.* New York: Palgrave Macmillan, 2015.

Bipartisan Policy Center and Association of American Colleges and Universities (AAC&U). "Is College Worth the Time and Money? It Depends on Whom You Ask." September 2021. https://bipartisanpolicy.org/download/?file=/wp-content/uploads/2021/09/BPC_Fed-State_Brief_R05.pdf.

Bloom, Allan. *The Closing of the American Mind: How Higher Education Has Failed Democracy and Impoverished the Souls of Today's Students.* New York: Simon and Schuster, 1987.

Boggs, Abigail, Eli Meyerhoff, Nick Mitchell, and Zach Schwartz-Weinstein. "Abolitionist University Studies: An Invitation." *Abolition*, August 28, 2019. https://abolitionjournal.org/abolitionist-university-studies-an-invitation/.

Brann, Eva T. H. *Paradoxes of Education in a Republic.* Chicago: University of Chicago Press, 1989.

Breneman, David. "Comments on the Spellings Commission Report: One Year Later." Forum for the Future of Higher Education | A Community of Academic Leaders and Scholars Who Explore New Thinking and Ideas in Higher Education, 2008. http://forum.mit.edu/articles/comments-on-the-spellings-commission-report-one-year-later/.

Butler, Judith. "Ordinary, Incredulous." In *The Humanities and Public Life*, edited by Peter Brooks and Hilary Jewett, 15–38. New York: Fordham University Press, 2014.

Butler, Paul. *Out of Style: Reanimating Stylistic Study in Composition and Rhetoric.* Logan: Utah State University Press, 2008.

Camp, Matthew J. "Books or Bombs?" *Inside Higher Ed*, September 14, 2021. https://www.insidehighered.com/views/2021/09/14/colleges-should-fight-investment-higher-ed-opinion.

Camper, Martin. *Arguing over Texts: The Rhetoric of Interpretation.* New York: Oxford University Press, 2018.

Chambliss, Daniel F. "The Flawed Metaphor of the Spellings Summit." *Inside Higher Ed*, April 5, 2007. https://www.insidehighered.com/views/2007/04/05/flawed-metaphor-spellings-summit.

Chaput, Catherine. *Inside the Teaching Machine: Rhetoric and the Globalization of the U.S. Public Research University*. Rhetoric, Culture, and Social Critique. Tuscaloosa: University of Alabama Press, 2008.

———. "Rhetorical Circulation in Late Capitalism: Neoliberalism and the Overdetermination of Affective Energy." *Philosophy and Rhetoric* 43, no. 1 (2010): 1–25.

Chávez, Karma R. "Beyond Inclusion: Rethinking Rhetoric's Historical Narrative." *Quarterly Journal of Speech* 101, no. 1 (2015): 162–72. https://doi.org/10.1080/00335630.2015.994908.

Cicero. *De Senectute De Amicitia De Divinatione*. Translated by William Armistead Falconer. Cambridge, MA: Harvard University Press, 1964. http://www.perseus.tufts.edu/hopper/text?doc=Perseus%3Atext%3A2007.01.0039%3Asection%3D17.

Cintron, Ralph. *Democracy as Fetish*. RSA Series in Transdisciplinary Rhetoric. University Park: Penn State University Press, 2020.

Clifton, Jennifer. "Casting Public Imagination for the Evolving Major." *Inside Higher Ed*, January 3, 2019. https://www.insidehighered.com/views/2019/01/03/academe-needs-cultivate-connection-between-imagination-and-public-life-opinion.

Cloud, Doug. "The Social Consequences of Dissociation: Lessons from the Same-Sex Marriage Debate." *Argumentation and Advocacy* 50, no. 3 (2014): 157–67. https://doi.org/10.1080/00028533.2014.11821816.

Coleman, Daniel, and Smaro Kamboureli, eds. *Retooling the Humanities: The Culture of Research in Canadian Universities*. Edmonton: University of Alberta Press, 2011.

Collini, Stefan. "Defending Universities: Argument and Persuasion." *Power and Education* 7, no. 1 (2015): 29–33. https://doi.org/10.1177/1757743814567383.

———. *What Are Universities For?* London; New York: Penguin, 2012.

"Commission on the Future of Higher Education." Accessed May 30, 2023. https://en.wikipedia.org/wiki/Commission_on_the_Future_of_Higher_Education.

"Community Think Tank." Department of English, Dietrich College of Humanities and Social Sciences, Carnegie Mellon University. Accessed February 6, 2022. http://www.cmu.edu/dietrich/english/courses/course-webpages/community-think-tank/index.html.

"Community Think Tank: Intercultural Problem Solving for Performance in Universities and WorkPlaces." n.d. http://www.cmu.edu/dietrich/english/courses/course-webpages/community-think-tank/index.html.

Cottom, Tressie McMillan. *Lower Ed: The Troubling Rise of For-Profit Colleges in the New Economy*. New York: New Press: 2018.

Craig, Ryan, and Allen Blue. *A New U: Faster + Cheaper Alternatives to College*. Dallas: BenBella Books, 2018.

Crosswhite, James. *Deep Rhetoric: Philosophy, Reason, Violence, Justice, Wisdom*. Chicago: University of Chicago Press, 2013.

Czerniewicz, Laura. "Unbundling and Rebundling Higher Education in an Age of Inequality." EDUCAUSE Review, October 29, 2018. https://er.educause.edu/articles/2018/10/unbundling-and-rebundling-higher-education-in-an-age-of-inequality.

Daniels, Ronald J., Grant Shreve, and Phillip Spector. *What Universities Owe Democracy*. Baltimore: Johns Hopkins University Press, 2021.

Davidson, Cathy N. *The New Education: How to Revolutionize the University to Prepare Students for a World in Flux*. New York: Basic Books, 2017.

Dewey, John. *The Quest for Certainty*. In *Later Works, 1925–1953*, edited by Jo Ann Boydston, vol. 4, 1929. Carbondale: Southern Illinois University Press, 2008.

Dorn, Charles. *For the Common Good: A New History of Higher Education in America*. Ithaca: Cornell University Press, 2017.

Dunmire, Patricia L. *Projecting the Future Through Political Discourse: The Case of the Bush Doctrine*. Discourse Approaches to Politics, Society and Culture 41. Amsterdam: John Benjamins, 2011.

Eberly, Rosa A. *Citizen Critics*. Urbana: University of Illinois Press, 2000.

———. "From Writers, Audiences, and Communities to Publics: Writing Classrooms as Protopublic Spaces," *Rhetoric Review* 18, no. 1 (1999): 165–78.

Ewell, Peter T. "Assessment and Accountability in America Today: Background and Context." *New Directions for Institutional Research* 2008, no. S1 (June 2008): 7–17. https://doi.org/10.1002/ir.258.

Fabricant, Michael, and Stephen Brier. *Austerity Blues: Fighting for the Soul of Public Higher Education*. Baltimore: Johns Hopkins University Press, 2016.

Fahnestock, Jeanne, and Marie Secor. "The Stases in Scientific and Literary Argument." *Written Communication* 5, no. 4 (1988): 427–43. https://doi.org/10.1177/0741088388005004002.

Fairclough, Norman. "Language and Neo-Liberalism." *Discourse and Society* 11, no. 2 (2000): 147–48. https://doi.org/10.1177/0957926500011002001.

Farrell, Thomas B. "Knowledge, Consensus, and Rhetorical Theory." *Quarterly Journal of Speech* 62, no. 1 (1976): 1–14. https://doi.org/10.1080/00335637609383313.

———. "Social Knowledge II." *Quarterly Journal of Speech* 64, no. 3 (1978): 329–34. https://doi.org/10.1080/00335637809383437.

Fester, Rachel, Marybeth Gasman, and Thai-Huy Nguyen. "We Know Very Little: Accreditation and Historically Black Colleges and Universities." *Journal of Black Studies* 43, no. 7 (2012): 806–19.

Field, Kelly. "A Texas Millionaire Plots the Future of Higher Education." *Chronicle of Higher Education*, June 2, 2006. https://www.chronicle.com/article/a-texas-millionaire-plots-the-future-of-higher-education/.

Fischer, Frank. *Reframing Public Policy: Discursive Politics and Deliberative Practices*. New York: Oxford University Press, 2003.

Fisher, Mark. *Capitalist Realism: Is There No Alternative?* Winchester, UK: Zero Books, 2009.

Fitzpatrick, Kathleen. *Generous Thinking: A Radical Approach to Saving the University*. Baltimore: Johns Hopkins University Press, 2019.

Fitzsimons, Patrick. "Managerialism and Education." In *Encyclopedia of Educational Philosophy and Theory*, edited by Michael Peters, 1–5. Singapore: Springer Singapore, 2015. https://doi.org/10.1007/978-981-287-532-7_341-1.

Flower, Linda. *Community Literacy and the Rhetoric of Public Engagement*. Carbondale: Southern Illinois University Press, 2008.

———. "Intercultural Knowledge Building: The Literate Action of a Community Think Tank." In *Writing Selves/Writing Societies: Research from Activity Perspectives*, edited by Charles Bazerman and David R. Russell, 239–79. Denver, CO: WAC Clearinghouse, 2003.

———. "Outcomes of Engaged Education: From Transfer to Transformation." In progress.

Flower, Linda, Elenore Long, and Lorraine Higgins. *Learning to Rival: A Literate Practice for Intercultural Inquiry*. Hoboken, NJ: Taylor and Francis, 2000.

Frank, David A. "Dialectical Rapprochement in the New Rhetoric." *Argumentation and Advocacy* 34, no. 3 (1998): 111–26.

Fraser, Nancy. "Rethinking the Public Sphere: A Contribution to the Critique of Actually Existing Democracy." *Social Text*, no. 25/26 (1990): 56–80. https://doi.org/10.2307/466240.

Gagliardi, J. S., et al. *American College Presidents Study 2017*. Washington, DC: American Council on Education, 2017.

Garahan, Katie L. "The Public Work of Identity Performance: Advocacy and Dissent in Teachers' Open Letters." *Rhetoric and Public Affairs* 22, no. 1 (2019): 59–94. https://doi.org/10.14321/rhetpublaffa.22.1.0059.
Gates Foundation. "Postsecondary Value Commission Report Proposes Action to Address Disparities in Economic Returns to College with Regard to Race, Income and Gender." May 2021. https://www.gatesfoundation.org/ideas/media-center/press-releases/2021/05/postsecondary-value-commission-findings.
Gavazzi, Stephen M., and E. Gordon Gee. *Land-Grant Universities for the Future: Higher Education for the Public Good.* Baltimore: Johns Hopkins University Press, 2018.
Goldrick-Rab, Sara, Drew M. Anderson, and Peter Kinsley. *Paying the Price: College Costs, Financial Aid, and the Betrayal of the American Dream.* Chicago: University of Chicago Press, 2016.
Goodnight, G. Thomas. "The Personal, Technical, and Public Spheres of Argument: A Speculative Inquiry into the Art of Public Deliberation." *Argumentation and Advocacy* 48, no. 4 (2012): 198–210. https://doi.org/10.1080/00028533.2012.11821771.
Gounari, Panayota. "Contesting the Cynicism of Neoliberal Discourse: Moving Towards a Language of Possibility." *Studies in Language and Capitalism* 1 (2006): 77–96.
Graff, Gerald, and Cathy Birkenstein. "A Progressive Case for Educational Standardization: How Not to Respond to the Spellings Report." *Academe* 94, no. 3 (2008): 16–18.
Green, Angela. "The Politics of Literacy: Countering the Rhetoric of Accountability in the Spellings Report and Beyond." *College Composition and Communication* 61, no. 1 (2009): W367–84.
Hariman, Robert. *Political Style: The Artistry of Power.* New Practices of Inquiry. Chicago: University of Chicago Press, 1995.
Harvey, David. *A Brief History of Neoliberalism.* Oxford: Oxford University Press, 2011.
Heifetz, Ronald A., Alexander Grashow, and Martin Linsky. *The Practice of Adaptive Leadership: Tools and Tactics for Changing Your Organization and the World.* Boston: Harvard Business Press, 2009.
Hillman, Nicholas, and Taylor Weichman. "Education Deserts: The Continued Significance of 'Place' in the Twenty-First Century." Viewpoints: Voices from the Field. Washington, DC: American Council on Education, 2016.
Hlavacik, Mark. *Assigning Blame: The Rhetoric of Education Reform.* Cambridge, MA: Harvard Education Press, 2016.
Horton, Scott. "Not for Profit: Six Questions for Martha Nussbaum." *Harper's Magazine,* June 1, 2010. https://harpers.org/2010/06/_not-for-profit_-six-questions-for-martha-nussbaum/.
Hull, Kathleen E. "The Political Limits of the Rights Frame: The Case of Same-Sex Marriage in Hawaii." *Sociological Perspectives* 44, no. 2 (2001): 207–32. https://doi.org/10.2307/1389611.
Huot, Brian. "Consistently Inconsistent: Business and the Spellings Commission Report on Higher Education." *College English* 69, no. 5 (2007): 512–25. https://doi.org/10.2307/25472233.
Institute for Higher Education Policy (IHEP). "IHEP Celebrates House Passage of College Transparency Act in the America COMPETES Act." Accessed March 13, 2022. https://www.ihep.org/press/americacompetes-act/.
Isocrates. *Isocrates II: On the Peace. Areopagiticus. Against the Sophists. Antidosis. Panathenaicus.* Translated by George Norlin. Loeb Classical Library 229. Cambridge, MA: Harvard University Press, 1929. Reprint, Cambridge, MA: Harvard University Press; London: William Heinemann Ltd, 1980.
Jameson, Fredric. "The Politics of Utopia." *New Left Review,* no. 25 (2004): 35–54.

Jaschik, Scott. "Gates Foundation Effort Releases New Tool to Compare Colleges." *Inside Higher Ed*, November 4, 2021. https://www.insidehighered.com/news/2021/11/04/gates-foundation-effort-releases-new-tool-compare-colleges.

———. "House Approves College Transparency Act." *Inside Higher Ed*, February 7, 2022. https://www.insidehighered.com/news/2022/02/07/house-passes-college-transparency-act.

Kanelos, Pano. "We Can't Wait for Universities to Fix Themselves. So We're Starting a New One." Substack Newsletter. Common Sense, November 8, 2021. https://bariweiss.substack.com/p/we-cant-wait-for-universities-to.

Kimball, Bruce A. *Orators and Philosophers: A History of the Idea of Liberal Education*. New York: College Entrance Examination Board, 1995. https://eric.ed.gov/?id=ED385485.

Kuehl, Rebecca A. "The Rhetorical Presidency and 'Accountability' in Education Reform: Comparing the Presidential Rhetoric of Ronald Reagan and George W. Bush." *Southern Communication Journal* 77, no. 4 (2012): 329–48. https://doi.org/10.1080/1041794X.2012.678926.

Kuh, George D. "Risky Business: Promises and Pitfalls of Institutional Transparency." *Change* 39, no. 5 (2007): 30–35. https://doi.org/10.3200/CHNG.39.5.30-37.

Labaree, David F. *A Perfect Mess: The Unlikely Ascendancy of American Higher Education*. Chicago: University of Chicago Press, 2017.

Lakoff, George. "Metaphor, Morality, and Politics, Or, Why Conservatives Have Left Liberals in the Dust." *Social Research* 62, no. 2 (1995): 177–214. https://escholarship.org/uc/item/7vp15113.

———. *Moral Politics: What Conservatives Know That Liberals Don't*. Chicago: University of Chicago Press, 1996.

Lakoff, George, and Mark Johnson. "Conceptual Metaphor in Everyday Language." *Journal of Philosophy* 77, no. 8 (1980): 453. https://doi.org/10.2307/2025464.

Lawrence University News. "Martha C. Nussbaum: Liberal Education Crucial to Producing Democratic Societies." June 11, 2013. http://blogs.lawrence.edu/news/2013/06/martha-nussbaum-liberal-education-crucial-to-producing-democratic-societies.html.

Lederman, Doug. "Testing, Testing." *Inside Higher Ed*, August 8, 2006. https://www.insidehighered.com/news/2006/08/08/testing-testing.

Lewis, Laurie K. *Organizational Change: Creating Change Through Strategic Communication*, 2nd ed. Foundations in Communication Theory. Chichester, UK: Wiley-Blackwell, 2019.

Liu, Ming. "'Contesting the Cynicism of Neoliberalism': A Corpus-Assisted Discourse Study of Press Representations of the Sino-US Currency Dispute." *Journal of Language and Politics* 16, no. 2 (2017): 242–63. https://doi.org/10.1075/jlp.15010.liu.

Long, Elenore. *A Responsive Rhetorical Art: Artistic Methods for Contemporary Public Life*. Composition, Literacy, and Culture. Pittsburgh: University of Pittsburgh Press, 2018.

Lorenz, Chris. "If You're So Smart, Why Are You Under Surveillance? Universities, Neoliberalism, and New Public Management." *Critical Inquiry* 38, no. 3 (2012): 599–629. https://doi.org/10.1086/664553.

Maher, Brent D. "Divided by Loyalty: The Debate Regarding Loyalty Provisions in the National Defense Education Act of 1958." *History of Education Quarterly* 56, no. 2 (2016): 301–30. https://doi.org/10.1111/hoeq.12184.

Markovits, Elizabeth. *The Politics of Sincerity: Plato, Frank Speech, and Democratic Judgment*. University Park: Penn State University Press, 2010.

Markwardt, Daylanne. "From Sputnik to the Spellings Commission: The Rhetoric of Higher Education Reform." PhD diss., University of Arizona, 2012. http://hdl.handle.net/10150/228460.

McIntush, Holly G. "Defining Education: The Rhetorical Enactment of Ideology in *A Nation at Risk*." *Rhetoric and Public Affairs* 3, no. 3 (2000): 419–43. https://doi.org/10.1353/rap.2010.0069.

McKenna, Bernard J., and Philip Graham. "Technocratic Discourse: A Primer." *Journal of Technical Writing and Communication* 30, no. 3 (2000): 223–51. https://doi.org/10.2190/56FY-V5TH-2U3U-MHQK.

McMahon, Walter W. *Higher Learning, Greater Good: The Private and Social Benefits of Higher Education*. Baltimore: Johns Hopkins University Press, 2009.

McMillan Cottom, Tressie. *Lower Ed: The Troubling Rise of For-Profit Colleges in the New Economy*. New York: New Press, 2018.

Medvetz, Thomas. *Think Tanks in America*. Chicago: University of Chicago Press, 2014.

Miller, Carolyn R. "Opportunity, Opportunism, and Progress: Kairos in the Rhetoric of Technology." *Argumentation* 8, no. 1 (1994): 81–96. https://doi.org/10.1007/BF00710705.

Mitchell, Brian Christopher, and W. Joseph King. *How to Run a College: A Practical Guide for Trustees, Faculty, Administrators, and Policymakers*. Baltimore: Johns Hopkins University Press, 2018.

Moen, Matthew C. "Aristotle in an Era of Accountability." Portland, OR, 2008. https://www.ccas.net/files/public/Moen_Presidential_Address_for_CCAS_website.pdf.

Montgomery, Beronda, and Joseph Whittaker. "Reimagining Academic Leadership." *ASBM Today*, July 6, 2021. https://www.asbmb.org/asbmb-today/opinions/070621/reimagining-academic-leadership.

Muckelbauer, John. *The Future of Invention Rhetoric, Postmodernism, and the Problem of Change*. Albany: State University of New York Press, 2009.

Muller, Jerry Z. *The Tyranny of Metrics*. Princeton: Princeton University Press, 2019.

National Endowment for the Humanities. "Martha C. Nussbaum Talks About the Humanities." Accessed February 27, 2022. https://www.neh.gov/humanities/2017/spring/conversation/martha-c-nussbaum-talks-about-the-humanities-mythmaking-and-international-development.

National Task Force on Civic Learning and Democratic Engagement and Association of American Colleges and Universities. *A Crucible Moment: College Learning and Democracy's Future*. Washington, DC: Association of American Colleges and Universities, 2012.

Nelson, Christopher. "Remarks for Ivory Tower Overhaul: How to Fix American Higher Ed." Washington, DC, 2006. https://www.cato.org/multimedia/events/ivory-tower-overhaul-how-fix-american-higher-ed.

Newfield, Christopher. *The Great Mistake: How We Wrecked Public Universities and How We Can Fix Them*. Critical University Studies. Baltimore: Johns Hopkins University Press, 2018.

Nussbaum, Martha C. Commencement Address. Colgate University, May 16, 2010. https://www.colgate.edu/news/stories/commencement-address-martha-c-nussbaum.

———. *Not for Profit: Why Democracy Needs the Humanities*. Updated ed. Public Square. Princeton: Princeton University Press, 2016.

Ohmann, Richard. "Historical Reflections on Accountability." *Academe* 86, no. 1 (2000): 24. https://doi.org/10.2307/40252332.

Owen-Smith, Jason. *Research Universities and the Public Good: Discovery for an Uncertain Future*. Innovation and Technology in the World Economy. Stanford: Stanford Business Books, 2018.

Pender, Kelly. *Being at Genetic Risk: Toward a Rhetoric of Care*. RSA Series in Transdisciplinary Rhetoric. University Park: Penn State University Press, 2018.

———. *Techne, from Neoclassicism to Postmodernism: Understanding Writing as a Useful, Teachable Art*. Lauer Series in Rhetoric and Composition. Anderson, SC: Parlor Press, 2011.

Perelman, Chaïm, and Lucie Olbrechts-Tyteca. *The New Rhetoric: A Treatise on Argumentation*. Notre Dame: University of Notre Dame Press, 2006.

Phillips, Kendall R. *Testing Controversy: A Rhetoric of Educational Reform*. Understanding Education and Policy. Cresskill, NJ: Hampton Press, 2004.

Postsecondary Value Commission. "About." April 25, 2019. https://www.postsecondaryvalue.org/about/.

———. "Equitable Value: Promoting Economic Mobility and Social Justice Through Postsecondary Education." May 2021. https://www.postsecondaryvalue.org/wp-content/uploads/2021/05/PVC-Executive-Summary-FINAL.pdf.

———. "Meet the Commission." https://postsecondaryvalue.org/members/.

Rai, Candice. *Democracy's Lot: Rhetoric, Publics, and the Places of Invention*. Rhetoric, Culture, and Social Critique. Tuscaloosa: University of Alabama Press, 2016.

Reitter, Paul, and Chad Wellmon. *Permanent Crisis: The Humanities in a Disenchanted Age*. Chicago: University of Chicago Press, 2021.

Ritivoi, Andreea Deciu. "The Dissociation of Concepts in Context: An Analytic Template for Assessing Its Role in Actual Situations." *Argumentation and Advocacy* 44, no. 4 (2008): 185–97. https://doi.org/10.1080/00028533.2008.11821689.

———. *Intimate Strangers: Arendt, Marcuse, Solzhenitsyn, and Said in American Political Discourse*. New York: Columbia University Press, 2014.

Roberts, John. "No One Is Perfect: The Limits of Transparency and an Ethic for 'Intelligent' Accountability." *Accounting, Organizations and Society* 34, no. 8 (2009): 957–70.

Roberts-Miller, Patricia. *Deliberate Conflict: Argument, Political Theory, and Composition Classes*. Carbondale: Southern Illinois University Press, 2007.

Roth, Michael S. *Beyond the University: Why Liberal Education Matters*. New Haven: Yale University Press, 2015.

Ruben, Brent D., and Richard De Lisi. *A Guide for Leaders in Higher Education: Core Concepts, Competencies, and Tools*. Sterling, VA: Stylus, 2017.

Ruben, Brent D., Laurie Lewis, Louise Sandmeyer, and Travis Russ. *Assessing the Impact of the Spellings Commission: The Message, the Messenger, and the Dynamics of Change in Higher Education*. Washington, DC: National Association of College and University Business Officers, 2008.

Rude, Carolyn D. "Toward an Expanded Concept of Rhetorical Delivery: The Uses of Reports in Public Policy Debates." *Technical Communication Quarterly* 13, no. 3 (2004): 271–88. https://doi.org/10.1207/s15427625tcq1303_3.

Schiappa, Edward. *Defining Reality: Definitions and the Politics of Meaning*. Rhetorical Philosophy and Theory. Carbondale: Southern Illinois University Press, 2003.

Spellings, Margaret. "Congress Digs a Moat Around Its Ivory Tower." Politico, February 6, 2008. https://www.politico.com/story/2008/02/congress-digs-a-moat-around-its-ivory-tower-008361.

———. "A National Dialogue: Commission on the Future of Higher Education." Prepared Remarks for Secretary Spellings at the Meeting of the Commission on the Future of Higher Education. Charlotte, NC, September 19, 2005. https://web.archive.org/web/20090322071446/https://www.ed.gov/news/speeches/2005/09/09192005.html.

Staley, David J. *Alternative Universities: Speculative Design for Innovation in Higher Education*. Baltimore: Johns Hopkins University Press, 2019.
"Student Loan Debt Clock." Accessed October 11, 2021. https://finaid.org/loans/studentloandebtclock/.
Styhre, Alexander. *Management and Neoliberalism: Connecting Policies and Practices*. New York: Routledge, 2018.
Sullivan, Dale L. "A Closer Look at Education as Epideictic Rhetoric." *Rhetoric Society Quarterly* 23, nos. 3–4 (1994): 70–89.
Tiede, Hans-Joerg. *University Reform: The Founding of the American Association of University Professors*. Baltimore: Johns Hopkins University Press, 2015.
Tilghman, Shirley. "2007 President's Commencement Remarks." Princeton University, 2007. https://www.princeton.edu/news/2007/06/05/2007-presidents-commencement-remarks.
Toth, Emily. "Regulating the New Consumerism." *Inside Higher Ed*, September 28, 2006. https://www.insidehighered.com/views/2006/09/28/regulating-new-consumerism.
Tracy, Karen. *Challenges of Ordinary Democracy: A Case Study in Deliberation and Dissent*. Rhetoric and Democratic Deliberation. University Park: Penn State University Press, 2010.
Turner, Cory. "President Obama's New 'College Scorecard' Is A Torrent Of Data." NPR, September 12, 2015, sec. Higher Ed. https://www.npr.org/sections/ed/2015/09/12/439742485/president-obamas-new-college-scorecard-is-a-torrent-of-data.
———. "Want to Find an Affordable College? There's a Website for That." NPR, February 17, 2022, sec. Education. https://www.npr.org/2022/02/15/1080773523/student-loans-financial-aid-tool-college-scorecard.
Union College. "Founders Day Speaker [Martha C. Nussbaum] Celebrates the Liberal Arts," February 24, 2011. https://www.union.edu/news/stories/201102/Founders-Day-speaker-celebrates-the-liberal-arts.
U.S. Congress. House. *America COMPETES Act of 2022*. HR 4521. 117th Cong., 2nd sess (February 28, 2022). https://www.congress.gov/bill/117th-congress/house-bill/4521.
U.S. Congress. *National Defense Education Program*. U.S. Code 20 (1958), §§ 401–589. https://www.loc.gov/item/uscode1958-004020017/.
U.S. Congress. Senate. *College Transparency Act*. S 839. 117th Cong., 1st Sess. (March 18, 2021). https://www.congress.gov/bill/117th-congress/senate-bill/839/text.
U.S. Department of Education. *A Nation at Risk: The Imperative for Educational Reform. An Open Letter to the American People. A Report to the Nation and the Secretary of Education*. Washington, DC: U.S. Department of Education, April 1983. https://eric.ed.gov/?id=ED226006.
———. *A Test of Leadership: Charting the Future of U.S. Higher Education*. Washington, DC: U.S. Department of Education, 2006. https://files.eric.ed.gov/fulltext/ED493504.pdf.
Vivian, Bradford. "Style, Rhetoric, and Postmodern Culture." *Philosophy and Rhetoric* 35, no. 3 (2002): 223–43. https://doi.org/10.1353/par.2003.0005.
Wan, Amy J. "In the Name of Citizenship: The Writing Classroom and the Promise of Citizenship." *College English* 74, no. 1 (2011): 28–49.
———. *Producing Good Citizens: Literacy Training in Anxious Times*. Pittsburgh Series in Composition, Literacy, and Culture. Pittsburgh: University of Pittsburgh Press, 2014.
Ward, David. "Current Concerns and Future Prospects of Higher Education in the United States." Remarks at the 4th EUA Convention of European Higher Education Institutions. Lisbon, Portugal, 2007.

Williams, Jeffrey. "Deconstructing Academe." *Chronicle of Higher Education*, February 19, 2012. https://www.chronicle.com/article/deconstructing-academe/.

———. "The Post-Welfare State University." *American Literary History* 18, no. 1 (2006): 190–216.

Winslow, Luke. "The Undeserving Professor: Neoliberalism and the Reinvention of Higher Education." *Rhetoric and Public Affairs* 18, no. 2 (2015): 201–45.

Wolfe, Joanna, Barrie Olson, and Laura Wilder. "Knowing What We Know About Writing in the Disciplines: A New Approach to Teaching for Transfer in FYC." *WAC Journal* 25, no. 1 (2014): 42–77. https://doi.org/10.37514/WAC-J.2014.25.1.03.

Young, Iris Marion. "Activist Challenges to Deliberative Democracy." *Political Theory* 29, no. 5 (2001): 670–90.

Zakaria, Fareed. *In Defense of a Liberal Education*. New York: W. W. Norton, 2016.

Zemsky, R. M. "The Rise and Fall of the Spellings Commission." 2007. https://repository.upenn.edu/cgi/viewcontent.cgi?article=1046&context=gse_pubs.

INDEX

Italicized page references indicate tables.

academic leadership style. *See* leadership style, academic
access, to higher education, 3, 35, 37, 40, 42, 51, 62–63, 68, 85, 93–95, 106, 121, 125
accountability, 2, 6–7, 9–10, 11–20, 30, 35, 39, 45–79, 78, 89–90, 101–2, 108–10
  dissociation of, 39–40
  and institutional complexity, 56–57
  metrics of, 86 (*see also* metrics)
  paradigms of, 43–44
  public v. market value, 39, 57
  rhetoric of, 29, 39–44
Adler-Kassner, Linda, 41, 52–53
advocacy, public, 5–11, 41, 77–79, 78–80, 84, 89–94, 93, 95, 99, 100, 105–6
  and dissociation, 44–45, 55–61
  and higher ed leaders, 105–9
  rhetoric of, 11–13, 21, 72
affordability. *See* higher education: cost of
Alexander, Lamar, 78, 108–10
Allen, Danielle, 87, 89
American Association of Colleges and Universities (AAC&U), 4, 63, 99
American Association of University Professors (AAUP), 64, 68–69, 74, 92, 93, 99
American Council on Education (ACE), 103
Asen, Robert, 5, 24, 42, 85, 89
Association of American Universities (AAU), 54–55
auditing, 24, 27–29, 32–34, 37
autonomy, of higher ed institutions, 3–4, 47, 51, 55–57, 66, 72, 76, 108, 111

Bennett, Douglas C., 46–47
Berdahl, Robert, 54
Bill and Melinda Gates Foundation, 3, 14, 57, 112, 115
Birkenstein, Cathy, 51, 52, 56, 67
Breneman, David, 63
briefing book, 97–98

Bush, George W., 6, 17
Butler, Judith, 7–8, 39, 76, 117–18

Chambliss, Daniel, 19, 30–32
Clifton, Jennifer, 78, 100
colleges and universities, for-profit, 73
colleges and universities, ranking, 55-56
colleges and universities, types of, 6
College Scorecard, 14, 41, 102–3, 106–12, 114
College Transparency Act, 14, 37, 107, 110–12, 116
Commission on the Future of Higher Education. *See* Spellings Commission
community think tank model, 94–99
COVID-19 epidemic, 121–22

"data-driven decision making," 117
Davidson, Cathy, 83
debt, student, 2, 48, 61, 72–73, 99, 103, 114. *See also* higher education: cost of; student loans
deliberation, 37, 74–75, 90, 94–116
democracy, 8, 12–13, 15, 20, 30–36, 39–40, 46, 50–52, 59, 62, 64–70, 74–77, 81–82, 85, 87, 90, 101, 104–5, 119
dissociation, 44–45
  external/internal authority, 52–53
  profit/pure motives, 53–55
  quantitative/qualitative, 48–50
  singular/plural missions, 46–48
  standardized/progressive, 50
  See also accountability: dissociation of
diversity, human, 14, 69–70, 74–75, 112–16
diversity, institutional, 5, 46, 57, 76

efficiency, 20, 24–25, 28–30, 32–34, 42, 86, 105, 110, 118
Elementary and Secondary Education Act, 42
Eliot, Charles, 83
elitism, 48, 56, 73–74

epideictic rhetoric, 47, 53, 76, 92, 119
equity, 39, 57, 82, 106, 112–16, 122
　See also diversity, human
expertise, 23, 27, 33, 43, 52–53, 68, 70, 73–74, 76, 84, 87, 96, 103, 118, 121–22

Field, Kelly, 17
Fitzpatrick, Kathleen, 59, 91–92
Flower, Linda, 94–95, 99–100
Frank, David, 45
funding, public, 2, 5, 8, 19, 25, 35, 39, 60–61, 72–73, 85, 93, 108, 110
futurism, 13, 24, 28–30, 32–34, 80, 81–84, 86

Garcia, Mildred, 112
Gardner, David Pierpont, 17
Gates Commission. See Postsecondary Value Commission
Gavazzi, Stephen M., 87
Gee, E. Gordon, 87
Goldrick-Rab, Sara, 8
Goodnight, Thomas, 122
Graff, Gerald, 51–52, 56, 67

Harrington, Susanmarie, 41, 52–53
Hatch, Orrin, 107
higher education, 2–3, 76, 82–84, 90
　advocacy for (see advocacy, public)
　cost of, 16, 72–73, 85
　criticisms of, 1–2, 5, 13–14
　economic value of (see value, economic)
　purpose of, 2, 31–32, 35, 49–51, 65–66
　social value of, 112–16
　and utilitarianism, 49
Higher Education Act (HEA), 61, 102, 107–10
Higher Education for American Democracy, 15
Hlavacik, Mark, 5, 19
humanities, 4, 7–10, 39, 52, 60–61, 63–64, 67, 69–70, 76, 81, 89, 91, 99–100, 112
Huot, Brian, 19, 30, 32

imagination, public, 70, 81–82, 84, 86, 88, 100
individualism, 47–48, 50, 55, 57, 61, 65–66, 69, 72–73, 113, 120
Institute for Higher Education Policy (IHEP), 107, 112
internal improvement paradigm, 43–44
Isocrates, 1, 3
ivory tower metaphor, 74, 93, 109

Johnson, Lyndon B., 42

Kamanetz, Anya, 48
Kanelos, Pano, 80
King, Joseph, 82–83
knowledge, making of, 2, 34, 46, 65, 68, 71, 74, 85, 92, 97, 121–22

Labaree, David, 3, 61–62, 114
leadership style, academic, 13, 20–24, 30–32, 32–34, 34
leadership style, managerial, 13, 20–24, 32–35, 33–34, 118
leadership style, realist, 20–22
learning, nature of, 31–32
Lederman, Doug, 31, 48
liberal arts, 4, 6, 8, 10, 44, 47–48, 50–51, 55, 59, 65, 69, 73, 75, 121
Long, Elenore, 98–99

managerial leadership style. See leadership style, managerial
market-based frame, 5–6, 13, 22, 24–26, 32–34, 42, 44, 60–61, 64–65, 73, 103, 106, 115, 119
Marr, Linsey, 122
McIntush, Holly, 42
McKlusky, Neal, 48
metaphors, competition, 29
metaphors, slowness, 29
metaphors, speed, 29
"metric fixation," 12, 20, 116–19
metrics, 3, 6–7, 20, 23, 27–28, 40, 43–44, 49–50, 53, 56, 75, 100, 103–4, 106, 110–12, 115–18
Miller, Charles, 17–19, 22, 31–32, 36, 48
Mitchell, Brian, 82–83
Modern Language Association (MLA), 51, 64, 67–70, 72
Moen, Matthew C., 54
Muller, Jerry, 27, 75, 103, 117–18

Nation at Risk, A, 15–16, 42
National Commission on Excellence in Education, 42
National Defense Education Act, 15
Nelson, Christopher, 31–32, 48–49, 50, 52, 64–67, 69, 72
neoliberalism, 20, 60, 118
New Public Management (NPM), 23
Newfield, Christopher, 8, 60, 62, 73
No Child Left Behind (NCLB), 15, 27, 51, 57
Nussbaum, Martha, 8, 64, 69–70

Ohmann, Richard, 41–42
Olbrechts-Tyteca, Lucie, 44–45, 63, 118–19

Owen-Smith, Jason, 82, 93, 102, 121–22

Perelman, Chaïm, 44–45, 63, 118–19
Plato, 65
Postsecondary Value Commission, 3, 112–16
privacy, student, 54, 111–12
public capacities, 59, 64
  deliberative, 68–70, 87
  ethical, 66–67
  technical, 68
public frame, 13, 33–34, 58, 59, 66–69, 71
  challenges to, 70, 75–76, 84, 90
  definition of, 64
  and Spellings report, 63–64
public good, 1–11, 30, 33–36, 39–40, 45, 57, 59–66, 68, 70–79, 81–82, 85–86, 90
  definition of, 2
  rhetorical approach to, 11–14
public sphere, 34, 51, 59, 62, 64, 68–69, 71, 72–75, 84–87

Reagan, Ronald, 15, 42
Reindl, Travis, 56
rhetoric, 4–6, 8–10
  dissociation types (*see* dissociation types)
  epideictic (*see* epideictic rhetoric)
  and futurism, 28, 32
  and higher ed accountability, 19–20, 39–44, 45–47, 55, 102
  and higher ed leadership, 9–12, 77–90, 91–95, 98–101, 118–19
  and higher ed policy, 4–7, 11–12
  and individual gain, 57
  and managerial style, 32–34, 37
  and the public frame, 59–66, 72, 76
  and Spellings report, 22–25, 29, 37
Roberts-Miller, Patricia, 71, 90, 101
Roth, Michael, 8
Ruben, Brent, 9–10, 47

Schiappa, Edward, 52, 62
social justice, 70, 114–15, 122
Socrates, 65–66
Spellings, Margaret, 6, 15–17, 37, 102, 109–10
Spellings Report, 6–7, 16
  and accountability, 35–36, 40–45, 45–52, 75–77
  approach of, 15–18, 22–23, 86, 102–3
  criticisms of, 19, 24, 30–31, 63–64

  and deliberation, 89
  and dissociation (*see* dissociation)
  and futurism, 28–30
  history of, 6–7
  misunderstanding of, 35–36
  and public advocacy, 92–93
  and public frame, 63–64
  and public good, 64–68, 68–70, 78–79, 99–101
  and quantification, 27–28
  results of, 106–12
  rhetoric of, 28–30, 32–35
  style of, 18–20, 23–24
Staley, David, 81–82
student loans, 72–73, 103, 114
See also debt, student

Test of Leadership, A. See Spellings Report
Tilghman, Shirley, 46–50
topoi, 11, 13, 45–55, 59, 119
Toth, Emily, 54, 110
transparency, 14, 20, 24, 27–30, 32–34, 44, 102, 105–12, 116
Truman, Harry S., 15
Truman Commission on Higher Education, 17, 35
Turner, Cory, 106
Twigg, Carol, 28

University of Austin, 80–81
U.S. Department of Education, 6, 34, 55–56, 106–11

value, economic, 62–63, 103, 104–5
  private, 6, 16–17, 26, 57
  public, 6, 57
Value Equity Explorer, 114
values, shared, 5–6, 65, 67, 73, 85
Voight, Mamie, 107
Voluntary Systems of Accountability, 41

Ward, David, 104
Warner, Michael, 84
Warren, Elizabeth, 107
Williams, Jeffrey, 61
Winslow, Luke, 60, 104

Young, Iris Marion, 74–75

Zook, George F., 17

RHETORIC AND DEMOCRATIC DELIBERATION

Other books in the series:

Karen Tracy, *Challenges of Ordinary Democracy: A Case Study in Deliberation and Dissent* / Volume 1

Samuel McCormick, *Letters to Power: Public Advocacy Without Public Intellectuals* / Volume 2

Christian Kock and Lisa S. Villadsen, eds., *Rhetorical Citizenship and Public Deliberation* / Volume 3

Jay P. Childers, *The Evolving Citizen: American Youth and the Changing Norms of Democratic Engagement* / Volume 4

Dave Tell, *Confessional Crises and Cultural Politics in Twentieth-Century America* / Volume 5

David Boromisza-Habashi, *Speaking Hatefully: Culture, Communication, and Political Action in Hungary* / Volume 6

Arabella Lyon, *Deliberative Acts: Democracy, Rhetoric, and Rights* / Volume 7

Lyn Carson, John Gastil, Janette Hartz-Karp, and Ron Lubensky, eds., *The Australian Citizens' Parliament and the Future of Deliberative Democracy* / Volume 8

Christa J. Olson, *Constitutive Visions: Indigeneity and Commonplaces of National Identity in Republican Ecuador* / Volume 9

Damien Smith Pfister, *Networked Media, Networked Rhetorics: Attention and Deliberation in the Early Blogosphere* / Volume 10

Katherine Elizabeth Mack, *From Apartheid to Democracy: Deliberating Truth and Reconciliation in South Africa* / Volume 11

Mary E. Stuckey, *Voting Deliberatively: FDR and the 1936 Presidential Campaign* / Volume 12

Robert Asen, *Democracy, Deliberation, and Education* / Volume 13

Shawn J. Parry-Giles and David S. Kaufer, *Memories of Lincoln and the Splintering of American Political Thought* / Volume 14

J. Michael Hogan, Jessica A. Kurr, Michael J. Bergmaier, and Jeremy D. Johnson, eds., *Speech and Debate as Civic Education* / Volume 15

Angela G. Ray and Paul Stob, eds., *Thinking Together: Lecturing, Learning, and Difference in the Long Nineteenth Century* / Volume 16

Sharon E. Jarvis and Soo-Hye Han, *Votes That Count and Voters Who Don't: How Journalists Sideline Electoral Participation (Without Even Knowing It)* / Volume 17

Belinda Stillion Southard, *How to Belong: Women's Agency in a Transnational World* / Volume 18

Melanie Loehwing, *Homeless Advocacy and the Rhetorical Construction of the Civic Home* / Volume 19

Kristy Maddux, *Practicing Citizenship: Women's Rhetoric at the 1893 Chicago World's Fair* / Volume 20

Craig Rood, *After Gun Violence: Deliberation and Memory in an Age of Political Gridlock* / Volume 21

Nathan Crick, *Dewey for a New Age of Fascism: Teaching Democratic Habits* / Volume 22

William Keith and Robert Danisch, *Beyond Civility: The Competing Obligations of Citizenship* / Volume 23

Lisa A. Flores, *Deportable and Disposable: Public Rhetoric and the Making of the "Illegal" Immigrant* / Volume 24

Adriana Angel, Michael L. Butterworth, and Nancy R. Gómez, eds., *Rhetorics of Democracy in the Americas* / Volume 25

Robert Asen, *School Choice and the Betrayal of Democracy: How Market-Based Education Reform Fails Our Communities* / Volume 26

Stephanie R. Larson, *What It Feels Like: Visceral Rhetoric and the Politics of Rape Culture* / Volume 27

Billie Murray, *Combating Hate: A Framework for Direct Action* / Volume 28

David A. Frank and Franics J. Mootz III, eds., *The Rhetoric of Judging Well: The Conflicted Legacy of Justice Anthony M. Kennedy* / Volume 29

Kristian Bjørkdahl, ed., *The Problematic Public: Lippman, Dewey, and Democracy in the Twenty-First Century* / Volume 30

Ekaterina V. Haskins, *Remembering the War, Forgetting the Terror: Appeals to Family Memory in Putin's Russia* / Volume 31